Lantzer

W9-DJH-153

THE ONE MINUTE BUSINESSMAN'S DEVOTIONAL

**Wisdom and Inspiration
for Today's Business Professional**

by
Mike Murdock

Tulsa, Oklahoma

Unless otherwise indicated, all Scripture quotations are taken from the *King James Version* of the Bible.

Scripture quotations marked AMP are taken from *The Amplified Bible, Old Testament.* Copyright © 1965, 1987 by The Zondervan Corporation, Grand Rapids, Michigan. Used by permission.

Verses marked TLB are taken from *The Living Bible,* copyright © 1971. Used by permission of Tyndale House Publishers, Inc., Wheaton, Illinois 60189. All rights reserved.

The One Minute Businessman's Devotional —
Wisdom and Inspiration for Today's Business Professional
ISBN 1-56292-045-6
Copyright © 1992 by Mike Murdock
P. O. Box 99
Dallas, Texas 75221

Published by Honor Books
P. O. Box 55388
Tulsa, Oklahoma 74155

Printed in the United States of America.
All rights reserved under International Copyright Law.
Contents and/or cover may not be reproduced in whole or in part in any form without the expressed written consent of the Publisher.

CONTENTS

PART I

HOW TO ENJOY THE WINNING LIFE

1
HOW TO ENJOY
THE WINNING LIFE

I love to see people *succeed* with their life.

And so does God, the Creator. As the artist treasures his painting, and the master craftsman the quality of the violin he created, so our Maker cherishes the dreams, goals, excellence of life and the happiness you and I are to enjoy.

Success is being happy. And, happiness is basically feeling good about yourself, your life, and your plans. Or, as my friend Kathy Alls says, "Success is *joy!*"

Two forces are vital to happiness: your *relationships* and your *achievements*.

The Gospel also has two forces: the *Person* of Jesus Christ, and the *principles* He taught. You see, one is the *Son* of God, the other is the *system* of God. One is the *life* of God, the other is the *law* of God. One is the *King*, the other is the *kingdom*. One is an *experience with God*, the other is the *expertise of God*. One is *heart*-related, the other is *mind*-related.

Salvation is experienced *instantaneously*, the Wisdom Principles are learned *progressively*.

Both forces are absolute essentials to total success and happiness.

You may be a *church member* and religious in your experience, but you will live in continuous periods of *frustration without the knowledge of the success laws established in the Scriptures.* The *expertise* of God is a must in situations that arise in our daily living.

You may be a *non*-church member, an unbeliever. You may experience tremendous social, financial and family success and achievements through simple application of the Laws of Life as set forth in the Bible. But without the *experience* with Jesus Christ, the Son of God, you will always sense a vast void and loneliness, an awareness that "something is missing in my life." Job promotion, financial empire building and social acceptance will heighten and accentuate the emptiness rather than fill it. *God has not created a world He would not be needed in.*

Through searching diligently for Principles for successful living, I was suddenly made aware of these *two forces,* the Person of Jesus and the Principles He set in motion. The *combined* power of these two influences I call the **"Way of the Winner."** The *system* I found in Scripture *worked.* It has multiplied my joy a thousand times over.

I wrote this book for *you.* I pray that each page will give the *added edge* you need to make your life happier than ever before.

Success is the *progressive achievement of God-intended goals.* It is attainment of the will and plans *of the Father.* It is important that we have a *dream* or purpose in our lives. Joseph dreamed a dream. Jesus had purpose.

WISDOM PRINCIPLE

A Productive Life
Is Not an Accident.

Our goals should be ordered of the Lord. David wanted to build the temple. But his desire was not a God-intended goal. Solomon was the builder God had chosen. Sometimes our personal desires are contradictory to God's plans.

How do we know the difference? *Consultation* with the Father. Through the *Word* and private prayer time, we discover God's plans. Usually, it is revealed step-by-step.

If your desire for something PERSISTS, it probably is an indication that God wants you involved in that particular accomplishment. For example, God chose Solomon to build, but David PREPARED the materials.

Obviously, we must *know* what God wants us to do *before* we can do it. LOOK for signs. LISTEN to the Spirit. Evaluate. Cultivate *instant response* to the Voice of God. *Eliminate the time-wasters* in your life. Concentrate on your God-connection.

Reject all feedback and comments that breed doubt and defeat. Jesus did not give the same quality time to the Pharisees that He gave to the Samaritan woman. He discerned the *purpose of every conversation,* whether it came from a hungry heart or a critical attitude.

The WINNER knows the power of words. Refuse to release words of defeat, depression and discouragement. Your words are life. Express hope and confidence in God. Get so excited over planning your triumphs, you don't have time to complain over past losses.

> **WISDOM PRINCIPLE**
>
> Never Speak Words
> That Make Satan
> Think He's Winning.

The WINNER expects opposition. Recognize that adversity has advantages. It reveals the depth of friendships. It will force you to dig for more accurate information. It will help you decide what you really believe.

> ┌─── **WISDOM PRINCIPLE** ───┐
> Adversity Is Breeding Ground
> for Miracles.

The WINNER expects special wisdom to come. "If any of you lack wisdom, let him ask of God, that giveth to all men liberally, and upbraideth not; and it shall be given him" (James 1:5). Wisdom is the *ability to interpret a situation through God's eyes.* Wisdom is seeing what God sees. Understanding and wisdom are the golden keys to mastering every circumstance in life. It comes through WORD STUDY. "The entrance of thy words giveth light; it giveth understanding unto the simple" (Ps. 119:130).

WINNERS are different from the "crowd." *Never* justify failure. Refuse to bog down in placing blame on others. *Reach UP for the key OUT.*

HAPPINESS BEGINS BETWEEN YOUR EARS. *Your mind is the drawing room for tomorrow's circumstances.* What happens in your mind will happen in time. *Mind-management* is first priority for the overcomer. "...Whatsoever things are true, whatsoever things are honest, whatsoever things are just, whatsoever things are pure, whatsoever things are lovely, whatsoever things are of good report; if there be any virtue, and if there be any praise, think on these things" (Phil. 4:8).

WISDOM PRINCIPLE

Those Who Are Unwilling To Lose,
Rarely Do.

Winners are simply ex-losers who got *mad*. They got tired of failure. The DAY YOU GET ANGRY AT YOUR FAILURES IS THE DAY YOU START WINNING. Winning doesn't start around you — it begins INSIDE you.

Circle today's date on your calendar. Declare that the happiest and most productive days of your life are beginning TODAY! Never, never, never quit. YOU MAY BE MINUTES FROM YOUR MIRACLE.

WHEN YOU MAKE UP YOUR MIND,
IT'S JUST A MATTER OF TIME!

PART II

MASTER SECRETS
FOR TOTAL SUCCESS

JESUS HAD SOMETHING OTHERS NEEDED

"Greater love hath no man than this, that
a man lay down his life for his friends."
John 15:13

Everyone has problems.

Your success and happiness in life depends on
your willingness to help someone solve their problem.
Successful people are simply problem solvers. A successful
attorney solves *legal* problems. Doctors solve *physical*
problems. The automobile mechanic solves *car*
problems.

Jesus was a Problem-Solver.

Thousands were burdened with guilt because of
their sins. Jesus offered *forgiveness.* Thousands were
spiritually starved. He said, "I am the Bread of Life."
Hundreds had bodies riddled with sickness and
disease. Jesus "went about doing good, and healing
all that were oppressed of the devil" (Acts 10:38). Many
were possessed with evil spirits. Jesus set them *free.*

Jesus had something others needed.

He solved their problems. That's why thousands
sat for days as He taught them concerning the laws
of God and how to have extraordinary relationships
with other people.

His products were boldly declared. Eternal life. Joy. Inner peace. Forgiveness. Healing and health. Financial freedom. Take an inventory of yourself. What do you have to offer someone? What do you *enjoy* doing? What would you attempt to do if you knew it was impossible to fail?

```
┌──────── WISDOM PRINCIPLE ────────┐
│                                  │
│        Everything God Created    │
│            Is a Solution         │
│            to a Problem.         │
│                                  │
└──────────────────────────────────┘
```

You are not an accident. God planned your birth. "Before I formed thee in the belly I knew thee; and before thou camest forth out of the womb I sanctified thee, and I ordained thee..." (Jer. 1:5).

Everything God makes is a solution to a problem. Every person God created is a solution to a problem. God wanted a love relationship. So, He created Adam. Adam was lonely. So, God created Eve. This is the golden thread that links creation.

Think of your *contribution* to another as an *assignment* from God. A lawyer is assigned to his client. A wife is *assigned* to her husband. Parents are *assigned* to their children. A secretary is *assigned* to her boss.

Your assignment is always to a person or a people.

For example, Moses was assigned to the Israelites. Aaron was assigned to Moses.

Your assignment will always *solve a problem.* So, your life is a solution to someone in trouble. Find those

18

who need you and what you have to offer. Build your life around that contribution.

Jesus did.

Prayer

Father, help me to be a problem-solver. Give me your eyes to find those who need me and help me identify how I can help them. Thank You for creating me to be a solution to a problem. In Jesus' Name.

JESUS BELIEVED
IN HIS PRODUCT

"Be thou diligent to know the state of thy flocks, and look well to thy herds."

Proverbs 27:23

Doubt is deadly.

Have you ever walked into a room and felt anger in the atmosphere? Have you ever walked into a room and felt love and energy and excitement? Of course. *Your thoughts have presence.* They are like currents movng through the air. Those thoughts are capable of *drawing people toward us, or driving people away from us.*

Your attitude is always sensed. You will never succeed in any business unless you really believe in that business. You must believe in the product you are promoting. *Your doubts will eventually surface.*

Look at the life of Jesus. He believed He could *change* people. He believed that His product would *satisfy* people. "Whosoever drinketh of this water shall thirst again: But whosoever drinketh of the water that I shall give him shall never thirst; but the water that I shall give him shall be in him a well of water springing up into everlasting life" (John 4:13b,14).

What makes you believe in your product? Product knowledge.

His product was life. "The thief cometh not, but for to steal, and to kill, and to destroy: I am come that they might have life, and that they might have it more abundantly" (John 10:10).

```
┌──────── WISDOM PRINCIPLE ────────┐
│                                  │
│    Whatever You Have Been Given  │
│       Is What Someone Needs.     │
│                                  │
└──────────────────────────────────┘
```

He saw the damaged products. He knew that He was their connection for repair. Nobody could take His place and He knew it. "My sheep hear my voice, and I know them, and they follow me" (John 10:27).

You must take the time and make the effort to *know your product*. It may bore you, or even seem unnecessary. You may be anxious to sell your product, pocket the profit and get on with your life. *But success just does not happen that way.*

A lawyer must study new laws. A doctor must keep well-read on the latest journals concerning the body and new diseases. A policeman has to study his weapons, the laws of his community, his rights and the mind-set of criminals. If he does not study this, he knows he is "a dead man in the streets." His life is on the line.

```
┌──────── WISDOM PRINCIPLE ────────┐
│  Information Breeds Confidence.  │
└──────────────────────────────────┘
```

Don't expect to succeed unless you are thoroughly informed about your product.

Are you discouraged by your present job? Are you feeling a bit hopeless? Then, I suggest that you ask yourself some real soul-searching and honest questions. How much *time* have you spent cultivating an awareness of your business? Do you *use* your product? How many hours each day have you *invested* in *becoming informed*? Are you so busy trying to "make a buck" that you really have not developed a powerful understanding and confidence in what you are doing?

Jesus was very busy. He was teaching, preaching, traveling, performing miracles, and mentoring the unlearned. But, He always took the time to get alone with His Father and renew His understanding of His Purpose, His Plan, and His Product. "My people are destroyed for lack of knowledge" (Hos. 4:6).

Jesus believed in His product.

Prayer

Father, thank You for placing inside of me diligence to know my product/service/career to its fullest extent. I know that You have given ideas and methods for helping other people; teach me to develop a powerful understanding and confidence in what I am promoting. In Jesus' Name.

JESUS NEVER MISREPRESENTED HIS PRODUCT

"Recompense to no man evil for evil.
Provide things honest in the sight of all men."
Romans 12:17

Liars are eventually exposed.

It may take weeks or even months, but the truth always surfaces. "He that covereth his sins shall not prosper" Prov. 28:13).

Anyone who does business with you wants the truth. The total truth. People fear misrepresentation.

Jesus had the greatest product on earth: salvation. He offered the human race an oportunity to have a relationship with God. He spoke of heaven and angels. "In my Father's house are many mansions: if it were not so, I would have told you" (John 14:2).

But, He never painted a distorted picture.

He warned His disciples of *persecution.*

"But beware of men: for they will deliver you up to the councils, and they will scourge you in their synagogues" (Matt. 10:17).

He spoke of their *afflictions.* "Then shall they deliver you up to be afflicted, and shall kill you: and ye shall be hated of all nations for my name's sake" (Matt. 24:9).

He spoke of *loneliness.* "The foxes have holes, and the birds of the air have nests; but the Son of man hath not where to lay his head" (Matt. 8:20).

Jesus believed in preparing people for any possible situation that could happen. He was honest. His teaching was far more than a "pie in the sky" philosophy.

WISDOM PRINCIPLE

Give Another What He Cannot Find Anywhere Else, and He Will Keep Returning.

Listen to the Apostle Paul. "Of the Jews five times received I forty stripes save one. Thrice was I beaten with rods, once I was stoned, thrice I suffered shipwreck, a night and a day I have been in the deep" (2 Cor. 11:24,25).

This certainly does not sound like the most ideal sales talk to a group of students in Bible School. Paul did not misrepresent his product either.

Jesus spoke to many people of the good things and the benefits of what He offered. But, He was also quick to talk to them about the *total* picture, so they would be prepared to face their trials.

Address the benefits. Focus on the advantages that your product or your business will offer to another person. But never forget *that an honest relationship is worth one hundred sales.*

Your integrity will always be remembered longer than your product.

Jesus was honest.

Prayer

Father, I ask You to help me develop and maintain a standard of truth and integrity. Strengthen me as I strive to be more like Jesus — sincere, honest and trustworthy. Thank You that You will uphold me as I reach for Your standards. In Jesus' Name.

JESUS WENT WHERE THE PEOPLE WERE

"For, brethren, ye have been called unto liberty; only use not liberty for an occasion to the flesh, but by love serve one another."
Galatians 5:13

Somebody needs you.

Go find them. Activate yourself. Move toward neighbors. Move toward the members of your family. Get on the telephone. Go ahead, write that brief note to that close friend. You may be shy, timid and even feel inadequate. But, you will not succeed in life unless you are connected to people.

Success involves people. People who enable you to succeed may not always come to you. In fact, they rarely do. *You must go to them.*

Why do you think there are newspaper machines on every corner, and soft drink machines are on every floor of a hotel?

Successful people are accessible.

You will never possess what you are unwilling to pursue.

Jesus knew this. He did not set up a throne in the middle of each city and say, "This is my palace. This is the only place you can see me." He went to the marketplace. He went to the boats of fishermen. He went to the synagogue. He went to the homes of the people. He went everywhere. He "went through the towns, preaching the gospel, and healing every where" (Luke 9:6).

He was reachable.

WISDOM PRINCIPLE

You Will Never Possess
What You Are Unwilling To Pursue.

What is keeping you from reaching out toward others? Is it an inward fear or dread that you may be rejected or turned down? Are you intimidated in some way? There is something far more important than any rejection: *Your dreams and goals.*

Successful people are reachers. They dread rejection, too. But, they believe their goal is worth it.

Jesus left comfort. He left the presence of angels and His heavenly Father. He willingly walked into an atmosphere that was unholy and imperfect. He stepped out of a magnificent and perfect kingdom and into a world that was confused, stained and deadly. But, He walked *into* the lives of those who needed Him.

He went where the people were.

Your dream is connected to people. Lawyers need clients. Doctors need patients. Singers need musicians. Salesmen need customers.

Jesus went where people were hurting. He went to the lame, the blind, the poor, the wealthy. He talked to the learned, the ignorant, the hungry, the thirsty.

So, start your People-List today. There are two kinds of people in your life: 1) Those who *already* know that you have something they need, and 2) those who do not *yet* know you have something they need.

Your People-List may include your relatives. Neighbors. Newspaper boy. Gardener. Dentist. Manicurist. Hairdresser. Landlord. Doctor. Lawyer.

There is a *Law of Relationship* that says every person is merely four people away from any other human on earth. Think of it! This simply means that you know Bill, who knows Judy, who knows Charles, who knows anyone else you would ever want to know. *You are already networked with the entire world.*

You simply have to get out of your house. Get out of your car. Go to the door. Reach for your telephone.

Success always begins somewhere.

Success always begins at some moment.

Success always begins with someone.

You must go where people are.

Jesus did.

Prayer

Lord, I praise You for Your magnificent creation of men and women! I ask that You help me to reach out to others around me with boldness and confidence as never before. I know that You have given me a plan and opportunity to reach people and succeed with them. In Jesus' Name.

JESUS TOOK TIME TO REST

"And on the seventh day God ended his work which he had made; and he rested on the seventh day from all his work which he had made."

Genesis 2:2

Fatigue can be costly.

One notable President of the United States knew this. He absolutely refused to make any major decisions after 4:00 in the afternoon. He knew that *a tired mind rarely makes good decisions.*

One bad decision can create countless tragedies.

Rest and recreation are not a sin. Rest time is *repair* time. It is *not* a loss of productivity. It is time for *renewing.* It is *receiving time.* It helps *release* your potential.

Jesus was an action man. A people person. He produced. He healed. He preached and taught. He walked among the people. *But He also knew the necessity of rest and relaxation. "*...Come ye yourselves apart into a desert place, and rest a while" (Mark 6:31).

Think about this. Daily, He faced hundreds of the sick and afflicted who screamed for His attention. Many were demon possessed. Mothers reached for Him. Fathers asked Him to pray for their children. Children did not want to leave His presence.

But, He *separated* Himself...*to receive.*

He knew that He could only give away that which He possessed. Work time is *giving.* Rest time is *receiving.* You must have both.

God created the earth in six days. But, He took the time to *rest* on the seventh day. He set an example for us. *Jesus did the same thing.*

```
┌────── WISDOM PRINCIPLE ──────┐
│         Faith Walks Out,     │
│    When Fatigue Walks in.    │
└──────────────────────────────┘
```

That might be the reason He was able to accomplish so much in three and a half years.

Life is demanding. People are demanding. In fact, the more you succeed, the more people will demand of you.

It is up to you to repair yourself.

Work hard. But, play just as enthusiastically. *Schedule it.* Take one day a week off completely. Totally relax. Focus on something completely different than your job. Your mind will think clearer. You will make better decisions. You will see life through different eyes. You will accomplish far more in less time.

Stop your frantic push for success. Take time to *taste the present.* The fires of desire will *always* rage within you. You must dominate that rage and focus it. *Learn to rest.*

Jesus did.

Prayer

Lord, teach me how to rest. Show me how I can turn towards You and refresh and rejuvenate myself. I know that without rest, I cannot accomplish the goals and desires that You have placed within me. Thank you for Your rest! In Jesus' Name.

JESUS TOOK TIME
TO PLAN

''Through skillful and godly Wisdom is a house [a life, a home, a family] built, and by understanding it is established [on a sound and good foundation]. And by knowledge shall the chambers [of its every area] be filled with all precious and pleasant riches.''

Proverbs 24:3,4 AMP

Champions plan.

Planning is the starting point for any dream or goal that you possess.

What is a plan? A plan is *a written list of arranged actions* necessary to achieve your desired goal. ''Write the vision, and make it plain upon tables, that he may run that readeth it'' (Hab. 2:2).

Jesus planned your future. ''In may Father's house are many mansions: if it were not so, I would have told you. I go to prepare a place for you'' (John 14:2).

Think for a moment. God scheduled the birth, the crucifixion, and resurrection of His Son before the foundation of the earth. ''And all that dwell upon the earth shall worship him, whose names are not written in the Book of Life of the Lamb slain from the foundation of the world'' (Rev. 13:8).

32

I think it is quite fascinating that God would schedule a meal, the marriage supper, six thousand years ahead of time! "Blessed are they which are called unto the Marriage Supper of the Lamb" (Rev. 19:9).

```
┌────────── WISDOM PRINCIPLE ──────────┐

          The Secret of Your Future
        Is Hidden in Your Daily Routine.

└──────────────────────────────────────┘
```

God always honored men who planned.

Noah *planned* the building of the ark. Solomon, the wisest man who ever lived on earth, *took time to plan* the building of the temple. Moses, the great deliverer, who brought the Israelites out of Egypt *took time to plan* the tabernacle.

Your Bible is the *plan of God* for you, the world, and eternity. It is the undeniable proof that God thinks ahead. Most of the Bible is prophecy, a description of the future before it ever occurs.

Jesus taught, "For which of you, intending to build a tower, sitteth not down first, and counteth the cost, whether he have sufficient to finish it? Lest haply, after he hath laid the foundation, and is not able to finish it, all that behold it begin to mock him, Saying, This man began to build, and was not able to finish. Or what king, going to make war against another king, sitteth not down first, and counsulteth whether he be able with ten thousand to meet him that cometh against him with twenty thousand?" (Luke 14:28-31).

Make a list of things to do every day of your life. Write six things you want to accomplish, that day. Focus your total attention on each task. Assign each task to a specific time. (If you cannot plan events for twenty-four hours in your life, what makes you think you will accomplish your desires for the next twenty-four years?)

Think of each hour as an employee. *Delegate a specific assignment to each hour.* What do you want to accomplish between 7 o'clock A.M. and 8 o'clock A.M.? Who should you telephone today?

Write out your plan clearly on a sheet of paper. *Successes are usually scheduled events.* Failures are not.

Planning is laborious. It is tedious. It is meticulous. It is grilling, demanding and exhausting. In my personal opinion, detailed planning is really never fun. *But sometimes you have to do something you hate to create something you love.*

Why do people avoid planning? Some avoid it because it is time consuming. They are so busy "mopping up the water" that they do not take the time to turn off the faucet!

The secret of your future is hidden in your daily routine.

Even ants think ahead. "Go to the ant, thou sluggard; consider her ways, and be wise: Which having no guide, overseer, or ruler, Provideth her meat in the summer, and gathereth her food in the harvest" (Prov. 6:6-8).

Jesus had a plan.

Prayer

Father, in Jesus' Name, I thank You for giving me the ability to plan. I ask that You give me wisdom in ordering my daily routine so that it allows me to get the most out of every hour.

Ingredient #1
Discern What Success Really Is*

---

*Throughout this devotional there will be ten ingredients for success.

JESUS KNEW THAT HE DID NOT HAVE TO CLOSE EVERY SALE TO BE A SUCCESS

"And let us not be weary in well doing: for in due season we shall reap, if we faint not."

Galatians 6:9

No simply means to "ask again".

Stop for a moment. Review your past experiences. You encountered rejection when you were a child. Some of your school mates may not have liked you. But you made it anyway, didn't you?

Rejection is not fatal. It is merely someone's opinion.

Jesus experienced more rejection than any human who ever lived on earth. He was born in a stable. He was born as an outcast in society. (Even today, television talk show hosts belittle and make fun of Him and those who follow Him. The Name of Jesus is used daily as a curse word by millions. His own people rejected him.)

"He came unto his own, and his own received him not" (John 1:11).

Did He quit? When Judas betrayed Him, did He allow Himself to become demoralized? No. *Jesus knew that He did not have to close every sale to be a success.* He went on to the others, who discerned His value. "But as many as received him, to them gave he power to become the sons of God, even to them that believe on his name" (John 1:12). He knew His *worth.* He knew His *product.*

```
┌─────── WISDOM PRINCIPLE ───────┐
        Sometimes You Have To
         Do Things You Hate
      To Create Something You Love.
└────────────────────────────────┘
```

He knew that critics died, but His plan was eternal.

Jesus was willing to experience a *season of pain,* to create an *eternity of gain. Some things last longer than rejection.* Your goals and dreams.

Move beyond your scars. Not everyone will celebrate you. Not everyone will welcome your future.

Someone needs what you have. Your contribution is an absolute necessity for their success. Discern it.

Pharisees rejected Jesus. The religious sect called Sadducees rejected Him. Religious leaders despised Christ. Those who should have recognized His worth wanted to destroy Him.

Jesus risked rejection to become the golden link between man and God.

Babe Ruth was famous for many yeas as the home run king in baseball history. Many people have never realized that he had more strike outs than any other batter also! They have not remembered his losses at bat. They merely remember his successes. He was willing to risk a strike out to hit that home run.

Most great salesmen say that knowing that fourteen out of fifteen people will say no, merely inspires them to hurry and make their presentations to as many as possible, to reach that one who will accept.

Jesus taught His disciples how to handle rejection. ''And whosoever shall not receive you, nor hear your words, when ye depart out of that house or city, shake off the dust of your feet'' (Matt. 10:14).

So, climb off your recliner. Make that telephone call. Write that letter.

Sooner or later you will succeed.

Jesus knew this.

Prayer

Lord, I thank You for Your faithfulness and reassurance in all times. Thank You for teaching me that I may sometimes be willing to experience a season of pain in order to receive a season of gain. You have given me the grace to do that which I do not like to do in order to achieve what I want. In Jesus' Name.

JESUS WAS A PROBLEM-SOLVER

"Let every one of us please his neighbour for his good to edification."

Romans 15:2

You were created to change somebody.

Every person you meet today is trying to *change* their life in some way. They desire excellence. They want *financial freedom*. They want their *health* to improve. They hate loneliness. You may not be sent to everyone, but you are definitely sent to someone.

You may not be qualified to help every person you meet. *But somebody needs something you possess.* It may be your warmth, your love, your gifts, or a special opportunity you can provide them.

Jesus understood this. He knew that He could *change* people for *good*. He possessed something that could eliminate sorrow and heartache from their life. He was a *Restorer*. He was a *Repairer*. "The thief cometh not, but for to steal, and to kill, and to destroy: I am come that they might have life, and that they might have it more abundantly" (John 10:10). Jesus understood the insatiable appetite for self-improvement and excellence.

WISDOM PRINCIPLE

You Can Only Conquer Your Past
by Focusing on Your Future.

There are four kinds of people in your life: those who add, subtract, divide, or multiply. Every relationship will affect you. For good or bad. *Those who do not increase you inevitably will decrease you.* ''He that walketh with wise men shall be wise: but a companion of fools shall be destroyed'' (Prov. 13:20). *Each relationship nurtures a strength or a weakness within you.*

Thousands of people want to *change*. They just don't know *how* to change. Every alcoholic hates his bondage. Most smokers long to quit. Drug addicts sit for hours wondering how they can break their chains of bondage.

Jesus looked for people in trouble. That's why He told His disciples that He needed to go through Samaria, where He met a woman with five marriages that had failed. He talked. She listened. He changed her life so permanently, that she went back into the city proclaiming the influence of Jesus in her life. *She conquered her past by focusing on her future.*

''But whosoever drinketh of the water that I shall give him shall never thirst; but the water that I shall give him shall be in him a well of water springing up into everlasting life'' (John 4:14). Jesus was water to the *thirsty.* He was bread to the *hungry.* He was a road map to the *lost.* He was a companion to the *lonely.*

Stop for a moment. What are your own greatest gifts? What is the *center of your expertise?* Are you a *good listener?* A good *speaker?* Whatever your gift is, that is what God will use to bless others through you.

Joseph had the ability to interpret dreams. Ruth took care of Naomi.

Your gift may not be needed by everybody. But it is definitely needed by *somebody.* Who are they? What is your gift? Whose life are you capable of improving today? Whose income could you improve? Whose peace of mind could you affect?

You are capable of motivating *somebody*. Maybe you can provide a climate, an atmosphere that unlocks the creativity of another. People want to succeed. People want to *improve*.

Someone has been waiting for you for a lifetime. They are worth pursuing. You are the golden thread missing in their life.

People want to *change*.

Jesus knew this.

Prayer

Thank You, Father, that You have placed within me a gift that is needed by someone in the world today. In Jesus' Name, I have been able to overcome my past by focusing on my gift and its possibilities. You have created me for a purpose.

JESUS WAS CONCERNED ABOUT PEOPLE'S FINANCES

"But my God shall supply all your need according to his riches in glory by Christ Jesus."

Philippians 4:19

Money is a reward.

Money is what you receive *when you help someone else achieve their goal.*

Payday is simply reward day. You are rewarded for spending your best hours of each day, your energy, and knowledge in helping your boss. He paid you for enabling him to reach his goal.

Money is very important. You cannot live in your home without it. You cannot provide for your family without it. Your automobile cost money. Your clothes cost money. Most marriage counselors observe that the number one cause of divorce is financial conflict.

Jesus recognized the importance of money.

Some think Jesus was a wandering nomad who wore a dirty white robe and sandals and who lived off scraps of food in the villages He visited. To the contrary, He had twelve men who handled His business. One was the treasurer. (John 13:29.)

WISDOM PRINCIPLE

Your Future Begins With
Whatever Is in
Your Hands Today.

Someone has said that Jesus talked more about money than heaven. In fact, twenty percent of His teaching and conversation was about talents, money and finances.

Jesus did not want you to worry about finances. "Therefore I say unto you, Take no thought for your life, what ye shall eat, or what ye shall drink; nor yet for your body, what ye shall put on. Is not the life more than meat, and the body than raiment? Behold the fowls of the air: for they sow not, neither do they reap, nor gather into barns; yet your heavenly Father feedeth them. Are ye not much better than they?" (Matt. 6:25,26).

Jesus knew that God loved to give people good things. "Every good gift and every perfect gift is from above, and cometh down from the Father" (James 1:17).

Money is a fact of life. It is necessary. You need it. Money is on God's mind. It is taught about in the Word of God.

God loves to see His people prosper. "Let the Lord be magnified, which hath pleasure in the prosperity of his servant" (Ps. 35:27).

God wants to reveal ways for you to profit and succeed financially. "I am the Lord thy God which teacheth thee to profit" (Isa. 48:17).

Jesus showed people *how to get ahead financially,* through His parables about using your gifts and talents. (Matt. 25:14-23).

Your future starts with whatever is in your hand today. Nothing is too little to multiply. Everything is *reproductive.* Everyone has received something from God capable of reproducing.

Jesus showed people that God was their true Source of everything. (Matt. 6:33.)

Jesus taught that giving was one of the ways to get ahead. "Give, and it shall be given unto you; good measure, pressed down, and shaken together, and running over, shall men give into your bosom. For with the same measure that ye mete withal it shall be measured to you again" (Luke 6:38).

Jesus taught the Law of Expectation that could unlock the 100-fold return. "But he shall receive an hundredfold now in this time, houses, and brethren, and sisters, and mothers, and children, and lands, with persecutions; and in the world to come eternal life" (Mark 10:30).

Jesus taught that you could give your way out of trouble. (Luke 6:38.)

Jesus taught fishermen where to drop their nets to catch fish. (Luke 5:1-10.)

Notice these incredible secrets: 1) Jesus visited people *where* they worked. 2) Jesus was so interested in their work that He instructed them as to the right time to drop their fishing nets and catch fish. 3) The disciples had enough confidence in Jesus' knoweldge that they went ahead and dropped their nets again in total obedience. 4) They caught more fish than they had ever caught, so much that their net broke. 5) Their success was so remarkable they had to have partners to help them pull in the fish. 6) When the disciples saw the incredible knowledge and concern and results of following Jesus' instructions, they realized how sinful they were, how limited they were. 7) They brought their ships to land, and decided to totally follow Jesus and His teachings. (Luke 5:11.)

Jesus took the time to show his disciples where to get money to pay their taxes. "Go thou to the sea, and cast an hook, and take up the fish that first cometh up; and when thou hast opened his mouth, thou shalt find a piece of money: that take, and give unto them for me and thee" (Matt. 17:27).

These are the facts: Jesus showed people *where* money could be found. He *motivated* them to *try* again and consider options and changes. He focused their mind on their *True Source*, the heavenly Father. He encouraged them to make *spiritual* matters a priority. Then, He encouraged them to look at their giving *as a seed*, linked to a *100-fold harvest*. He encouraged them to *expect a harvest* from everything they sowed into others and into God's work.

If there is one thing more exciting than "making money," it is helping others discover financial freedom, too.

Jesus did.

Prayer

Father, I trust You and rely upon You as the source for my every financial need. Help me to fully grasp that the key to receiving finances is to give finances away, no matter the amount. Please teach me how I can also show others how to discover financial freedom. In Jesus' Name.

JESUS WAS WILLING TO GO WHERE HE HAD NEVER BEEN BEFORE

"Also I heard the voice of the Lord, saying, Whom shall I send, and who will go for us? Then said I, Here am I; send me."

Isaiah 6:8

Geography makes a difference.

Pineapples do well in Hawaii. They do not do very well in Alaska. *Atmosphere matters.* The climate is important for any seed to grow.

You too, are a seed. Your business and your product are like seeds. It is true that you may need to change locations and situations to unlock the full potential of your success.

Success requires people. You will never succeed without networking with many different kinds of people. They may not be accessible. You may have to leave the comforts of your home to reach them to achieve extraordinary success.

Recently, I was amazed by what I saw in the life of Jesus. He was constantly in *movement,* constantly *changing* locations.

"...He was come down from the mountain..." (Matt. 8:1). "He entered into Capernaum..." (8:5).

46

"He went to...come into Peter's house..." (8:14).
"...He was entered into a ship..." (8:23). "And
when He was come to the other side into the country
of the Gergesenes..." (8:28).

```
┌─────── WISDOM PRINCIPLE ───────┐
│                                │
│      You Must Be Willing To Go │
│    Where You Have Never Been,  │
│       To Create Something You  │
│          Have Never Had.       │
│                                │
└────────────────────────────────┘
```

Jesus was constantly arising, departing, and going
to new places. He sought to be around new people.
He discussed His teaching with many types of people
of varied backgrounds.

Some people will not come to where you are. You
have to go to their home, their town and their
environment.

Once, Jesus told His disciples to go to the upper
room. They were to tarry there until they received the
marvelous experience of the Holy Spirit. He told five
hundred this. Three hundred eighty disobeyed Him.
Even after they had observed His resurrection and His
miracle life, only one hundred and twenty out of the
five hundred actually followed His instruction. But,
those who were willing to go to a different place — the
Upper Room, received the marvelous outpouring of
the Holy Spirit.

Abraham, the patriarch of the Israelites, had to
make *geographical changes* before his success was
birthed. (Gen. 12:1,2.)

Joseph found his incredible success in *another country*, Egypt.

Ruth willingly left her heathen family in Moab, and went to Bethlehem with Naomi where she met a Boaz, a financial giant of the community, and married him.

It is normal to move toward those who are easily accessible.

Sometimes you have to go somewhere you have never been before, before you taste the extraordinary success that you want to experience.

Jesus did.

Prayer

Father, I know that You have a plan for me. I ask that You help make me willing to go where I have never been before in order that You can help create the success that I have never experienced before. In Jesus' Name.

JESUS NEVER ALLOWED WHAT OTHERS SAID ABOUT HIM TO CHANGE HIS OPINION OF HIMSELF

"Blessed are ye, when men shall hate you, and when they shall separate you from their company, and shall reproach you, and cast out your name as evil, for the Son of man's sake. Rejoice ye in that day, and leap for joy: for, behold, your reward is great in heaven: for in the like manner did their fathers unto the prophets."

Luke 6:22,23

Nobody really knows you.

Consider this for a moment. Almost everyone in your life is more preoccupied with themselves than you. Therefore, you know more about yourself than anyone who will ever meet you. Never forget this.

It is not what men say about you that realy matters in life. *It is what you believe about yourself.*

Jesus was slandered. He was falsely accused. They said He was possessed with devils. Countless accusations were hurled like stones against Jesus every day of His life. But, it never affected Him.

He knew what He was really about. He believed in Himself. He believed in His product. He knew that His accusers were ignorant, unlearned and arrogant. He knew they simply feared Him.

```
┌──────────  WISDOM PRINCIPLE  ──────────┐
│                                         │
│        The Ammunition Selected          │
│            by Your Enemy                │
│      Is a Clue to His Fear of You.      │
│                                         │
└─────────────────────────────────────────┘
```

People always fight what they do not understand. *The mind will always resent what it cannot master.* Wars are fought because of ignorance and fear. Throughout human history, champions have had their names soiled and stained. Accusations and slanderous lies have come against great political leaders as well as ministers. This is life. Daniel was accusedof breaking the law. Joseph was falsely accused of raping his employer's wife. Paul was accused of arousing mobs through hatred and division concerning their belief systems of religious people.

Jesus never begged anyone to believe in Him. He knew that *integrity cannot be proven, it must be discerned.*

He never wasted time with critics. He kept His attention on His goal. *He stayed focused.*

They accused Jesus of being filled with devils. He paid no attention. He simply continued to cast out devils. (Matt. 12:24.)

Jesus never strived to ''look good.'' *He simply was good.* He did not labor to appear truthful. *He was truthful.* He never struggled to have a good reputation. *He had character.*

┌─── **WISDOM PRINCIPLE** ───┐

Integrity Cannot Be Proved;
It Must Be Discerned.

└─────────────────────────────┘

Every successful man wants to be loved, admired. But, your enemies and critics will never leave your reputation unstained and untarnished. You must rise above that fact. You must never allow what others say about you to change your personal opinion of yourself. *Never.*

Jesus did not.

Prayer

I pray, Lord, that I will not waste time concerning myself with what others say about me. In Jesus' Name, I thank You for the strength and faithfulness to not fall into an appearance of good or integrity, but to be a person of good, truth and character.

JESUS UNDERSTOOD TIMING AND PREPARATION

"By faith Noah, being warned of God of things not seen as yet, moved with fear, prepared an ark to the saving of his house."

Hebrews 11:7a

Prayer

Father, thank You for teaching me that champions aren't made, but they are recognized. With Your strength, I can make time my servant and prepare with excellence so that my performance reflects excellence. In Jesus' Name.

Champions never hurry.

The quality of preparation determines the quality of performance.

A great concert pianist invests hundreds of hours of practice before their concert. They know that the quality of those many grueling hours of practice will prepare him for his greatest performance. The world champion heavyweight boxer knows that he cannot wait to get into the ring with his opponent to prepare. It would be too late. So, for many weeks before the great fight, he toils with his morning workout, running and exercise program.

Champions do not *become* champions in the ring. They are merely *recognized* in the ring. Their *becoming,* happens in their *daily routine.*

Jesus never hurried.

Jesus did not begin His earthly ministry until He was thirty years old. His ministry was a short three and one half years. *His preparation time was thirty years.*

Jesus was very sensitive about timing. When His mother told Him that the people had run out of wine at the marriage of Cana, He replied, ''Woman, what have I to do with thee? mine hour is not yet come'' (John 2:4).

Jesus never hurried.

```
┌──────── WISDOM PRINCIPLE ────────┐
│      Every Season Has a Product.      │
└──────────────────────────────────┘
```

Several years ago, a friend of mine had just entered business. He was so excited about its remarkable potential. However, he did not want to spend time in learning how to present the plan to others. He felt it was just ''too detailed.'' As I watched him stumble over and over in his conversations with others, I finally said, ''Learn the business. Study the products. Take time to learn the details. *If you will take the time to prepare, your presentation will have believability.* The people will have confidence in becoming a part of your business. You may not learn all the details the first night you hear them, but don't worry; set aside some hours each week to begin to prepare your presentation.''

Preparation time is never wasted time.

It will take time to know your business. It will take time to know your product. It will take time to develop a list of customers and clients.

Think about the life of Jesus. He saw hundreds die around Him because of sickness and disease. But His time had not come. he saw thousands warped with the traditions and legalism of religious systems. But He knew that His Father was growing Him up. "And Jesus increased in wisdom and stature, and in favour with God and man" (Luke 2:52). Jesus was willing to wait.

He *prepared* Himself.

Ingredient #2
Set Definite Goals For Yourself

JESUS DEVELOPED A PASSION FOR HIS GOALS

"And whatsoever ye do, do it heartily, as to the Lord, and not unto men."

Colossians 3:23

Passion is power.

You will never have significant success with anything *until it becomes an obsession with you.* An obsession is when something *consumes* your thoughts and time.

You will only be remembered in life for your obsession. Henry Ford, the automobile. Thomas Edison, inventions. Billy Graham, evangelism. Oral Roberts, healing. The Wright brothers, the airplane.

Jesus had a passion for His mission and goal in life. "For the Son of man is come to seek and to save that which was lost" (Luke 19:10). "How God anointed Jesus of Nazareth with the Holy Ghost and with power: who went about doing good, and healing all that were oppressed of the devil; for God was with him" (Acts 10:38).

Jesus focused on doing the exact instructions of His heavenly Father. He healed the sick. He noticed the lonely. He came to make people successful, to restore and repair their life to full fellowship with His Father.

┌─────── **WISDOM PRINCIPLE** ───────┐

You Will Only Have Significant
Success With Something That
Is an Obsession.

└────────────────────────────────────┘

That obsession took Him to the cross. It took Him to
the crucifixion. Eight inches of thorns were crushed
into His brow. A spear punctured His side. Spikes
were driven into His hands. Thirty-nine stripes of a
whip tore His back to shreds. Four hundred soldiers
spit on His body. His beard was ripped off His face.
But He was *obsessed with the salvation of mankind.*

And He succeeded.

You may start small. You may start with very little.
But, if what you love begins to consume your mind,
your thoughts, your conversation, your schedule, look
for extraordinary success.

Do you dread going to work every morning? Do
you anxiously look at the clock toward closing time
each afternoon? Is your mind wandering throughout
the day toward other places or things you would love
to be doing? Then you will probably not have much
success at what you are doing.

Find something that consumes you. Something that
is worthy of building your entire life around. Consider it.

Jesus did.

Prayer

Father, I know that unless I set my heart upon a
goal, I will not accomplish it. I ask that You give me
the diligence and wisdom to turn Your goal into my
strongest desire. I will only get out of something what
I have put in it. In Jesus' Name.

JESUS RESPECTED AUTHORITY

"Servants, be obedient to them that are your masters according to the flesh, with fear and trembling, in singleness of your heart, as unto Christ; Not with eyeservice, as menpleasers; but as the servants of Christ, doing the will of God from the heart."

Ephesians 6:5,6

Authority creates order.

Imagine a nation without a leader. A work place without a boss. An army without a general. Authority creates order, *the accurate arrangement of things.* That is why you do not park your car in your bathroom! You do not eat your meals in the garage! There is a place and a time for everything.

Respect those in authority over you. Your success is affected by it. Honor those who have lived before you. They possess a wealth of knowledge. Listen. Learn. Observe them.

Mentorship is the Master Key to extraordinary success.

Jesus understood this. He was the Son of God. He knew more than any other human on earth. Yet, He honored the authority of His own government. When people came to Him, questioning His opinion of paying taxes to Caesar, He answered, "Render to

Caesar the things that are Caesar's, and to God the things that are God's" (Mark 12:17).

Are you speaking words of doubt about your own business? Are you belittling or criticizing your up-line? Stop it now. True, those in authority may not be perfect. They make mistakes. (Maybe that's why they can tolerate you! If they were perfect, they may not want to have any communication with you either!)

```
┌────── WISDOM PRINCIPLE ──────┐
│                              │
│     You Will Never Be Promoted     │
│  Until You Become Over-Qualified  │
│     for Your Present Position.     │
│                              │
└──────────────────────────────┘
```

If you are rebelling against every instruction given to you, then do not complain when those around you begin to rebel against your words and opinions. Learn to honor and respect those in authority over you.

Jesus did.

Prayer

Father, I know that respect for authority comes straight from Your Word. I ask that You remind me at every turn that success at my present position depends largely upon my respect and attitude towards those in leadership over me. I pray that You will be with them and honor them in all they do. In Jesus' Name.

JESUS NEVER DISCRIMINATED

"These things also belong to the wise. It is not good to have respect of persons in judgment."

Proverbs 24:23

Treat people right.

Some years ago, Elvis Presley did a concert in Indianapolis, Indiana. One of my close friends, a deputy sheriff, in Indianapolis, was in charge of security backstage. He noticed that a man was walking around dressed in an old windbreaker jacket. He was shuffling around as if he were some bum off the street. As my friend prepared to evict him from the building, someone stopped him and said, "That man is Colonel Parker, the manager of Elvis Presley." He was shocked and stunned. He had misjudged the man because of his appearance.

Stop prejudging people. Your first impression is always limited. It is possibly very wrong. *Only fools make permanent decisions without knowledge.* Never assume your intuition or perception is always correct.

Your success in business will be affected by prejudice, fear and any discrimination you allow.

Jesus never discriminated because of someone's race, sex or financial status.

He was comfortable in the presence of fishermen, or with the tax collectors of His day. He was at ease with men or women, the rich and the poor.

WISDOM PRINCIPLE

Nobody Is Ever as They
First Appear.

You see, *Jesus knew that everybody contained potential.* He never eliminated someone just because of their past. Born of a mother who conceived Him as a virgin, He knew what it meant to have a questionable background. He rose above it.

Jesus broke tradition. When the Samaritans were considered a lower class of people, and Jews would not even talk to them, Jesus did. in fact, He took the time to discuss with the woman at the well her entire life and *how He could change it.*

Peter said it this way, "Of a truth I perceive that God is no respecter of persons" (Acts 10:34).

James wrote it this way, "For if there come unto your assembly a man with a gold ring, in goodly apparel, and there come in also a poor man in vile raiment; And ye have respect to him that weareth the gay clothing, and say unto him, Sit thou here in a good place; and say to the poor, Stand thou there, or sit here under my footstool: Are ye not then partial in yourselves, and are become judges of evil thoughts?" (James 2:2-4).

Never eliminate anyone from the chain of your success.

Jesus refused to discriminate.

Prayer

Father, I know that You have created all people and that they are equal in Your sight. Thank You for giving me the wisdom to not condemn or pre-judge someone solely on first impressions. I trust in Your patience and discernment to see true character and intentions, not simply appearance. In Jesus' Name.

JESUS OFFERED INCENTIVES

"And, behold, I come quickly; and my reward is with me, to give every man according as his work shall be."

Revelation 22:12

Reward those who help you succeed.

People are motivated by two forces: Pain or pleasure. Fear or reward. Loss or gain.

For example, you may ask your child to mow the lawn. He sulks and complains, "But Daddy, I don't really want to mow the lawn today. I want to go play with my friends."

You have two ways to motivate him: pain or pleasure. Fear or incentive. Loss or gain. For instance, you may say, "Then son, bend over. I will have to discipline you with my belt." That is the *pain* motivation.

Or, you may use the *reward system.* "Son, I know you do not feel like doing it. But, if you do it, I will pay you $10." That is *incentive.* Reward. Gain.

Jesus used both methods to motivate.

In Luke 16, Jesus used fear motivation on the Pharisees who ridiculed Him. He described to them how the rich man went to hell and was "tormented in this flame" (v. 24).

However, when Jesus was talking to His disciples, He used *rewards and incentives* to motivate them. "In my Father's house are many mansions: if it were not so, I would have told you. I go to prepare a place for you'' (John 14:2,3).

— WISDOM PRINCIPLE —

You Will Always Move Toward Anyone Who Increases You and Away From Anyone Who Makes You Less.

You are created with a desire to *increase. Decrease is unnatural.* Remember, every person you meet today has an *appetite for increase.* They want to be benefited. There is nothing wrong with that. There is a God-given command on the inside of each person. . .to become more. *To multiply.* (Gen. 1:28.)

Carefully examine the benefits that you offer to others. Who *needs* your product? *Why* do they need it? What *problem* will your product *solve in their life?* What do you offer others *that they cannot find anywhere else?*

Study the incentives of your present business. Know them "like the palm of your hand."

People never buy your product for the reasons *you* sell it. They buy products *for what it will do for them.*

David asked what rewards would come to him if he killed the giant Goliath. He was told simply that he would never have to pay taxes again, and he would be able to marry the king's daughter. He took five stones. He killed the giant. *He had motivation. He had an incentive.*

People do things for different reasons. Interrogate. Interview people. Ask questions. Find out what their greatest needs are. Dig to discover what their greatest fears may be.

Remember, you are there *to solve a problem*. Take the time to show others "what is in it for them." Make sure they understand the rewards and benefits of conducting business with you.

Jesus did.

Prayer

Father, You have made me a problem-solver. I know that me or my product is designed to solve other people's problems. You have created me to increase, and help others avoid decrease by helping them increase too. Thank You for this ability. In Jesus' Name.

JESUS OVERCAME THE STIGMA OF A QUESTIONABLE BACKGROUND

"Brethren, I count not myself to have apprehended: but this one thing I do, forgetting those things which are behind, and reaching forth unto those things which are before, I press toward the mark for the prize of the high calling of God in Christ Jesus."

Philippians 3:13,14

Your past is over.

Are you having self-doubts today? This is common. Your limited education. Your father dying when you were young. An alcoholic parent. Guilt over a serious mistake you made in your teenage years. It is very important that you remember your past is over.

Never build your future around your past.

Jesus was born with a terrible stigma. His mother Mary, was pregnant with Him before she ever married Joseph, His father. The Bible says that they had not had a sexual relationship, but, "that which is conceived in her is of the Holy Ghost" (Matt. 1:20).

Only two people in the world really knew that Mary was a virgin: God and Mary.

Undoubtedly, hundreds of people mocked and sneered at Joseph for marrying Mary.

Jesus grew up with this. He stepped out of a cesspool of human scorn. He clawed His way out of a pit of questions. He ignored the slanderous remarks. He knew the truth. He knew who He was and what He was about. It did not matter that others did not believe. *He chose to chart His own course.* The opinions of others did not matter.

```
┌──────  WISDOM PRINCIPLE  ──────┐
│                                │
│   God Never Consults Your Past │
│     To Determine Your Future.  │
│                                │
└────────────────────────────────┘
```

He never looked back. He never discussed the situation with anyone. There is not a single Scripture in the entire Bible where He ever brought up His background or His limitations.

You too, can move beyond the scars of yesterday. Stop talking about your limited education. Quit complaining that everyone in your family is poor. Stop repeating stories of those who failed you. Stop pointing your fingers at the economy.

Stop advertising your pain. Stop meditating on your flaws. Everyone has limitations. Each of us are handicapped in some way. Physically. Emotionally. Mentally. Spiritually.

```
┌──────  WISDOM PRINCIPLE  ──────┐
│                                │
│  Stop Looking at Where You Have│
│    Been and Start Looking at   │
│      Where You Are Going.      │
│                                │
└────────────────────────────────┘
```

Concentrate on your *future*.

Jesus did.

Prayer

Thank You, Father, for Your Son who died on the cross and removed my past. You do not look at my past to determine my future. I know that if I rely upon You and concentrate on my future, my success is determined. In Jesus' Name.

JESUS NEVER WASTED TIME ANSWERING CRITICS

"Go from the presence of a foolish man, when thou perceivest not in him the lips of knowledge."

Proverbs 14:7

Critics are spectators, not players.

Critical people are usually disheartened people who have failed to reach a desired goal. Someone has said, "criticism is the death gargle of a non-achiever."

There has never been a monument built to a critic.

Critical people are *disappointed* people. *Disillusioned* people. *Unfocused* people. They are hurting inside. They build their life trying to destroy others.

Move away from them.

Don't get me wrong, debate is a marvelous arena. Conflict unlocks my energy.

But there is a place to present facts. There is a time for exchange of information. Constructive suggestions are always pursued by champions.

But there is a time *for silence.*

When Jesus was being ridiculed, and prepared for His crucifixion, He was silent. "But Jesus held His peace" (Matt. 26:63). Jesus did not feel obligated to answer critics. He never wasted time on people who were obviously trying to trap Him. He responded to *hunger*. He responded to *thirst*. He responded to *reachers*.

┌─── **WISDOM PRINCIPLE** ───┐

Never Spend More Time on a Critic Than You Would Give to a Friend.

└────────────────┘

You owe nothing to a critic. "Speak not in the ears of a fool: for he will despise the wisdom of thy words" (Prov. 23:9).

Criticism is deadly.

Correction is life.

Criticism is pointing out your flaws.

Correction is pointing out your potential.

Many years ago I sat down at my kitchen table to reply to a critical letter from a lady. I toiled over my reply. I erased words, and wrote new sentences. It took me over one hour of exhausting work to carefully carve out a decent reaction to her letter. I still wasn't satisfied with my answer to her. Suddenly I began to laugh as a thought dawned. It suddenly hit me that I had never spent an entire hour writing a letter to my own mother, the dearest person in the world to me. I had never spent one hour writing to the woman who had carried me within her womb for nine months, provided comfort and food during my life, motivated me toward God and to learn to play the piano. I had not spent that much time on the most important person in my life. I was a fool to spend that much time on a critic.

Jesus ignored the critics.

Prayer

Lord, I know that the time I spend answering critics is time wasted. I ask that You give me the strength and maturity to rise above those who are critical, and invest time in those whom I love and care for. In Jesus' Name.

Ingredient #3
Make Your Goals
Balanced and Reasonable

JESUS KNEW THERE WAS A RIGHT TIME AND A WRONG TIME TO APPROACH PEOPLE

''See then that ye walk circumspectly, not as fools, but as wise, Redeeming the time, because the days are evil. Wherefore be ye not unwise, but understanding what the will of the Lord is.''

Ephesians 5:15-17

There is a time for everything.

There is a right time to approach people.

Suppose you want a raise. You really want to discuss it with your boss and what you can do to be worth more to him. If you have just made a terrible mistake that has cost the company $15,000.00, that is not the right time to approach him about your raise. If the company has just experienced incredible profits because of an idea that you shared with your boss, that might be the proper climate and atmosphere to discuss it with him.

Jesus understood timing. He spent 30 years preparing for His ministry before He launched His first miracle. When His mother told Him that they had no wine at the wedding Jesus responded to her, "Mine hour is not yet come" (John 2:4).

There is a time to ask for forgiveness, there is a time to be silent. There is a time to make presentations to people. There is a time to wait.

People are in different seasons of their life. Moods change. Circumstances affect our decisions. *Be sensitive to this.*

```
┌──────── WISDOM PRINCIPLE ────────┐
│                                   │
│        Your Entry Can Decide      │
│          How You Exit.            │
│                                   │
└───────────────────────────────────┘
```

It is a rare husband who can anticipate the moods, and needs of his wife and react appropriately. It is a brilliant teenager who knows and understands proper timing in discussing problems with his parents.

Jesus understood timing. When they caught the woman in the act of adultery His reaction was unique. "And Jesus said unto her, Neither do I condemn thee: go, and sin no more" (John 8:11).

He did not ignore her sin. He did not ignore the accusatory tone of the men wanting to trap her. He simply knew there was a proper time to do things. He did not dissect the woman's sin. He did not unravel the details of the adulterous act. He never dwelled on the past, but pointed people toward their future. There was a time for that.

"To everything there is a season, and a time to every purpose under the heaven. He hath made everything beautiful in His time. . ." (Eccl. 3:1,11).

Your success depends on *timing*. Don't forget it. Whether you sell to a customer, or sit at the discussion table with your supervisor. Stay sensitive to others. Observe. Watch. Listen to the flow of information and what is going on.

Jesus did.

Prayer

Father, Your Word says that for each and every thing there is a season. I pray that You grant me the wisdom to recognize the proper timing for all that I do. Please bless me with the understanding that how I enter a situation can decide how I leave it. In Jesus' Name.

JESUS EDUCATED THOSE HE MENTORED

"Give instruction to a wise man, and he will be yet wiser: teach a just man, and he will increase in learning."

Proverbs 9:9

You will always remember what you teach.

Someone has said that you don't learn anything when you talk. You only learn when you listen. That is inaccurate. Some of my greatest thoughts and ideas have surfaced while I was teaching others.

It is very important that you mentor someone. Train them. Teach them what you know. Especially those over whom you have authority — any person who is carrying out an instruction for you, employees, children, or whoever.

Successful businesses have employees who are informed, well trained and confident about carrying out their instructions. This takes time. It takes energy. It takes great patience.

Every song needs a singer. Every achiever needs motivation. Every student needs a teacher.

Jesus was a master teacher. He taught thousands at a time. Sometimes, He sat with His twelve disciples and fed information into them. He kept them motivated, influenced and inspired.

He taught them about prayer. (Matt. 26:36-46.) He taught them about heaven. (John 14:2-4.) He taught them about hell. (Luke 16:20-31.) He educated His staff on many topics including His death, giving, and relationships.

```
┌──────── WISDOM PRINCIPLE ────────┐
│                                  │
│     You Will Always Remember     │
│       What You Teach.            │
│                                  │
└──────────────────────────────────┘
```

Jesus taught in synagogues. (Luke 13:10.) He also taught in the villages. (Mark 6:6.)

Here is the point. None of us were born with great knowledge. You became what you are. You *discovered* what you know. It took time, energy, and learning.

Your staff will not know everything. They may not see what you see. They may not feel what you feel. They may not have discovered what you know.

You must invest time to nurture their vision, their product knowledge and the rewards you want them to pursue.

You need good people around you. You need *inspired* people around you. You need *informed* people around you. You may be their *only* source for information and motivation.

Jesus educated His staff. Jesus constantly motivated the people He led by showing them the future of their present commitment.

Take the time to train others.

Jesus did.

Prayer

Father, just as Jesus educated His disciples, I choose to educate my staff. Thank You for revealing to me the most effective means of teaching and training those around me. I know that without a successor, there is no success. In Jesus' Name.

JESUS REFUSED TO BE DISCOURAGED WHEN OTHERS MISJUDGED HIS MOTIVES

> "The words of the wicked are to lie in wait for blood: but the mouth of the upright shall deliver them."
>
> Proverbs 12:6

Everyone has been misjudged.

When a minister speaks on prosperity, he risks being accused of greed. When he prays for the sick, he risks being called a fraud and a fake.

Your own family may misjudge your motives. Any person who carries out instructions for you may misjudge your actions.

Your boss might misread you. Customers may doubt your sincerity.

Don't be discouraged by that. Take the time to discuss your position with those who appear genuinely sincere. Do not waste your time and energy on those who are merely stirring up conflict.

Jesus was constantly misjudged by others. Pharisees accused Him of even being possessed by evil spirits. "But when the Pharisees heard it, they said, This fellow doth not cast out devils, but by Beelzebub the prince of the devils" (Matt. 12:24). Let me make a few suggestions. When you speak to others, be concise.

79

Be bold but very distinct in what you say. Do not leave room for misunderstandings when possible.

WISDOM PRINCIPLE

False Accusation Is the
Last Stage Before
Supernatural Promotion.

Let me make a few suggestions. *Always be where you are.* When you are in conversation with someone, totally focus on that conversation. Shut out everything else. When you totally focus on what you are saying and hearing, you do not have to reflect later on with regret about that conversation. This can prevent unnecessary misjudgment.

Every extraordinary achiever has been misjudged. People laughed over the thought of a horseless carriage. Others sneered when the telephone was invented.

Your success is on the other side of scorn and false accusations.

Jesus knew this.

Prayer

Father, thank You for redeeming situations in which others are critical or falsely accuse me. I rest in knowing that as I pattern myself after Jesus in ignoring my accusers, I will reach the other side of adversity — success. In Jesus' Name.

JESUS REFUSED TO BE BITTER WHEN OTHERS WERE DISLOYAL OR BETRAYED HIM

"Finally, be ye all of one mind, having compassion one of another, love as brethren, be pitiful, be courteous: Not rendering evil for evil, or railing for railing: but contrariwise blessing; knowing that ye are thereunto called, that ye should inherit a blessing."

1 Peter 3:8,9

Bitterness is more devastating than betrayal.

Betrayal is external. Bitterness is internal. You see, betrayal is something that *others do to you*. Bitterness is something you do to yourself.

Thousands survive betrayal easily. Very few can survive the currents of bitterness. "Looking diligently lest any man fail of the grace of God; lest any root of bitterness springing up trouble you, and thereby many be defiled" (Heb. 12:15).

Disloyalty is a product of an unthankful heart. Betrayal is usually the child of jealousy.

Everybody has experienced these tragic situations in their life. An unfaithful mate, an employee who slanders you behind your back. A boss who fires you without explanation. These things hurt. Deeply.

Jesus was at supper with His disciples. "And as they sat and did eat, Jesus said, 'Verily I say unto you, One of you which eateth with me shall betray me' " (Mark 14:18). Jesus knew *who* would betray Him. He knew *when* He would be betrayed. Yet, He saw something *more important* than the hurt and wounds of betrayal.

```
┌────── WISDOM PRINCIPLE ──────┐
│                              │
│   Injustice Is Only as Powerful as   │
│        Your Memory of It.         │
│                              │
└──────────────────────────────┘
```

Read Mark 14:43-50 and you will see one of the most demoralizing experiences any human can experience. Judas betrayed Him with a kiss.

Yet Jesus refused to be bitter.

Neither did He penalize Judas. Judas destroyed himself. He did not disconnect from Peter who denied Him. Peter cried out for mercy and forgiveness. He was restored and became the great preacher on the Day Of Pentecost.

"Let all bitterness, and wrath, and anger and clamor, and evil speaking, be put away from you, with all malice: And be ye kind one to another, tender hearted, forgiving one another, even as God for Christ's sake hath forgiven you" (Eph. 4:31,32).

Eliminate any words of bitterness in every conversation. Do not remind others of your experience unless it is to teach and encourage them to rise above their own hurts.

Jesus saw the chapter beyond betrayal.

He refused to be bitter.

Prayer

Thank You, Lord, for removing any bitterness from my heart. I will be on guard against bitterness in the future and will remember that when I am betrayed or judged unjustly, I can look past the hurt and see that bitterness is only a roadblock to success. In Jesus' Name.

JESUS NETWORKED WITH PEOPLE OF ALL BACKGROUNDS

"The heart of the prudent getteth knowledge; and the ear of the wise seeketh knowledge."

Proverbs 18:15

Greatness is everywhere.

People have different contributions. I believe you need different kinds of input into your life. Someone needs what you possess. You need something that they can contribute to you. You are the sum total of your experiences.

Personalities differ. Each person around you contains a different body of knowledge. It is up to you to "drop your pail in their well," and draw it out. "Where no counsel is, the people fall: but in the multitude of counsellors there is safety" (Prov. 11:14).

Look at those who surrounded Jesus. A tax collector. A physician. Fishermen. A woman who had been possessed with seven devils.

Some were poor. Some were wealthy. Some were very energetic while others were passive. Some were explosive like Peter. Others, like James, were logical.

Be willing to listen to others. Everyone sees through different eyes. They feel with different hearts. They hear through different ears. *Someone knows something that you should know.* You will not discover it until you take the time to stop and hear them out. *One piece of information can turn a failure into a success.* Great decisions are products of great thoughts.

```
┌─────── WISDOM PRINCIPLE ───────┐
│                                │
│       Pay Any Price To Stay    │
│         in the Presence of     │
│       Extraordinary People.    │
│                                │
└────────────────────────────────┘
```

Jesus networked.

Prayer

I realize, Lord, that Your creation is filled with many extraordinary and different people. Give me the wisdom and ability to recognize that who I spend my time with is time invested in my success. In Jesus' Name, I rely upon You as my source.

JESUS RESISTED TEMPTATION

"The Lord knoweth how to deliver the godly out of temptations...."

2 Peter 2:9a

Everybody is tempted.

Temptation is the presentation of evil. It is an opportunity to choose temporary pleasure rather than permanent gain.

You will experience many seasons during your life. During your teenage years, you may feel overwhelming currents of lust toward immorality. In your business world, you will be tempted to distort the truth, cheat on your taxes or even "pocket extra money for yourself." Unfaithful mates are epidemic. Billboards boldly declare their invitation to alcohol. Drugs are on every corner. Cocaine appears to be an escape, to many, from the complexities of life.

Satan is a master artist.

Jesus experienced a relentless and persistent adversary, the devil. It happened after He had fasted forty days and forty nights. His defense was quite simple: the written WORD OF GOD. "Then was Jesus led up of the Spirit into the wilderness to be tempted of the devil. And when he had fasted forty days and forty nights, he was afterward an hungred. And when the tempter came to him, he said, If thou be the Son of God, command that these stones be made bread. But he answered and said, 'It is written, Man shall not live by bread alone, but by every word that proceedeth out of the mouth of God.' Then the devil taketh him up into the holy city, and setteth him on a pinnacle of the temple, And saith unto him, If thou be the Son of God, cast thyself down: for it is written, He shall give his angels charge concerning thee: and in their hands they shall bear thee up, lest at any time thou dash thy foot against a stone. Jesus said unto him. 'It is written again, Thou shalt not tempt the Lord thy God.' Again, the devil taketh him up into an exceeding high mountain, and sheweth him all the kingdoms of the world, and the glory of them; And saith unto him, All these things will I give thee, if thou wilt fall down and worship me. Then saith Jesus unto him, 'Get thee hence, Satan: for it is written, Thou shalt worship the Lord thy God, and him only shalt thou serve.' Then the devil leaveth him, and behold, angels came and ministered unto him" (Matt. 4:1-11).

WISDOM PRINCIPLE

One Night of Pleasure Is Not
Worth a Lifetime of Blindness.

The graveyard is full of people who failed to resist satan. The prisons are overcrowded with people too weak to stand against him. Dreams crash daily on the rocks of temptation.

Move the ship of your life away from those rocks. Ask Samson and he will tell you, "One night of pleasure is not worth a lifetime of blindness."

Fight Back.

Jesus did.

Prayer

Father, I know that when I am tempted, I must boldly stand upon the Word of God. With Your strength, I can resist evil and not sacrifice my future for the present. In Jesus' Name, I have the conviction to do what is right.

Ingredient #4
Meditate On Scripture

JESUS MADE DECISIONS THAT CREATED A DESIRED FUTURE INSTEAD OF A DESIRED PRESENT

''That ye be not slothful, but followers of them who through faith and patience inherit the promises.''

Hebrews 6:12

Decisions create events.

If you eat two slices of pecan pie every night, what is the inevitable eventuality? If you smoke two packs of cigarettes daily, what is the inevitable eventuality? Everything you are presently doing will benefit your *present* . . . or your *future*. The choice is yours.

You will make a lot of decisions today. Some of them will pleasure you today. But tomorrow you will be miserable over those decisions. Some of those decisions may make you a little uncomfortable for today. But, tomorrow, you will be thrilled.

Tonight you will sit down at supper. Your mouth will water at the beautiful chocolate cake someone has prepared. You will make a decision about that chocolate cake. If you eat it, it will taste good for now. Tomorrow morning you will feel it and be unhappy with yourself for not refusing it. If you look at that piece of cake and say, ''I'm going to make a decision that *benefits my future.* I refuse it.'' That is the decision of a champion.

┌─────── **WISDOM PRINCIPLE** ───────┐

Make Decisions That Will
Create the Future You Desire.

└────────────────────────────────────┘

Jesus could have called ten thousand angels to deliver Him from the crucifixion. He was capable of coming down off of the cross. But, He made the decision in the garden of Gethsemane that created an incredible future. *He was willing to go through a season of pain to create an eternity of gain.*

''For our light affliction, which is but for a moment, worketh for us a far more exceeding and eternal weight of glory'' (2 Cor. 4:17).

Those who can wait, usually win. Those who refuse to wait, usually lose. Patience is powerful. It is productive.

Reprogram your thinking to distance. Reprogram your life for endurance. Start thinking ''long term'' about your eating habits. Your prayer life. Your friendships.

Jesus was a ''long termer.''

Prayer

In Jesus' Name I commit myself to thinking for the long term and not the short term. I know that each and every decision I make has an impact upon my future. Thank You, Father, for giving me the wisdom to make decisions that create my desired future.

91

JESUS NEVER JUDGED PEOPLE BY THEIR OUTWARD APPEARANCE

"My brethren, have not the faith of our Lord Jesus Christ, the Lord of glory, with respect of persons."

James 2:1

Nobody is ever as they first appear.

Packaging is deceptive. Cereal boxes make drab cereal look like the most exciting food in the world. Billions of dollars are spent on packaging.

Don't get me wrong. Clothing is very important. Appearance sells or discourages. Proverbs 7 talks about the clothing of a prostitute. Proverbs 31 describes the clothes of a virtuous woman. Most assuredly, *it is wise to create a climate of acceptance.* Naomi, the mentor of Ruth, instructed her to put on perfume and change her clothes before she went to meet Boaz, her future husband.

But, something is more important than the packaging. *The person.*

Jesus saw a scarred and weary woman who had been married five times. He saw beyond her failures and reputation. He saw her *heart.* He saw a *desire to be changed.* She was the golden bridge for Jesus to walk into the hearts of many of those people of her city. "And many of the Samaritans of that city believed on him for the saying of the woman, which testified, He told me all that ever I did" (John 4:39).

┌─── **WISDOM PRINCIPLE** ───┐

Nothing Is Ever as It First Appears.

└────────────────────────────┘

People saw Zaccheus as a conniving, deceptive tax collector. Jesus saw a confused man who longed for a change of heart. People of Israel saw in Absalom a handsome, articulate leader. He was a traitor and liar. Samson thought Delilah was the most beautiful woman he had ever met. She was the trap that destroyed his championship status.

An interesting story was shared recently by a friend of mine in Florida. She owns a clothing store. She said, "I have had ladies come to my store who looked like they did not have a penny to their name, yet purchase thousands of dollars worth of clothing, get into their chauffeured limousine and drive off. You could not tell what they possessed by what they wore."

Nothing is ever as it first appears.

Start listening for attitudes in people. Start listening for hurts. Don't misjudge them.

Jesus knew this.

Prayer

Father, I ask for the maturity to not judge others by their appearance, but to focus on their heart and how I can affect them. Lord, You have given us the compassion to reach others. Help me to help them. In Jesus' Name.

JESUS RECOGNIZED THE LAW OF REPETITION

"And these are they which are sown on good ground; such as hear the word, and receive it, and bring forth fruit, some thirtyfold, some sixty, and some an hundred."

Mark 4:20

What you hear repeatedly, you eventually will believe.

Teachers know that the basic law of learning is *repetition.* Someone has said you must hear something sixteen times before you really believe it.

Notice the television commercials. You have seen the same ones repeatedly. Billboards advertise well-known soft drinks over and over again. Why? You must *keep hearing* something, seeing something, before you respond to it.

It simply takes *time* to absorb a message.

Jesus taught people same truths again and again. "Then spake Jesus AGAIN unto them. . ." (John 8:12).

Someone taught you everything you know today. You are the result of a *process.* There was a time in your life that you could not even spell the word "cat." You did not know numbers. But somebody was patient with you.

Great achievers understand the necessity of teaching those around them — *again and again.*

```
┌─── WISDOM PRINCIPLE ───┐
│                        │
│  What You Hear Repeatedly, │
│  You Will Eventually Believe. │
│                        │
└────────────────────────┘
```

Don't expect those who are networked with you to understand everything instantly. You did not. They will not either. It takes time to grow greatness.

Jesus knew this.

Prayer

Lord, I know that what I continually hear is what I will eventually believe. Please teach me how I can avoid the negative aspects of hearing defeat, but that I can put this principle to use for Your glory and my success. In Jesus' Name.

JESUS WAS A TOMORROW THINKER

"Remember ye not the former things,
neither consider the things of old."
Isaiah 43:18

Become a *"tomorrow thinker."*

One of the great companies in Japan has a detailed plan for the next 100 years. They are *tomorrow thinkers.*

Jesus was a tomorrow thinker. When He met the Samaritan woman at the well, He barely mentioned that she had been married five times. *He pointed her to her future.* He said that He would give her water and she would never thirst again.

Another remarkable illustration of tomorrow thinking concerns the woman caught in the act of adultery. He never discussed her sin. He simply said unto her, "Neither do I condemn thee: go, and sin no more" (John 8:11).

"Remember ye not the former things, neither consider the things of old. Behold, I will do a new thing; now it shall spring forth; shall ye not know it? I will even make a way in the wilderness, and rivers in the desert" (Isa. 43:18,19).

WISDOM PRINCIPLE

Those Who Created Yesterday's
Pain Do Not Control
Tomorrow's Potential.

Satan discusses your past. That appears to be the only information he has. Jesus discusses your *future*. He enters your life to end your past and give birth to tomorrow.

Stop taking journeys into yesterday.

Jesus concentrated on the future.

Prayer

Father, I thank You that You have given me a new beginning. Thank You for pointing me to my future success. You have wiped my heart clean, and I will now move forward and not dwell on what was, but what is to come. In Jesus' Name.

JESUS KNEW THAT MONEY ALONE COULD NOT BRING CONTENTMENT

"Charge them that are rich in this world, that they be not highminded, nor trust in uncertain riches, but in the living God, who giveth us richly all things to enjoy."

I Timothy 6:17

Rich people are not always happy people.

Your hands can be full of money. Your head can be full of information. But if your heart is empty, your life is very empty.

Money is for movement, not accumulation. That is why the Bible talks about "the deceitfulness of riches."

Jesus saw this. He talked to the rich. He looked into their eyes and saw a longing for *something that money could not buy.* They came to Him late at night, when the crowds were gone. They were lonely. "...For a man's life consisteth not in the abundance of the things which he possesseth" (Luke 12:15).

Solomon was a wealthy king. Yet he confessed, "Therefore I hated life..." (Eccl. 2:17).

WISDOM PRINCIPLE

Prosperity Is Having Enough of
God's Provision To Complete
His Purpose for Your Life.

Think for a moment. You probably possess more today than any time in your whole life. Do you feel more joy than you've ever had in your life? Do you laugh more now than you've ever laughed? Do you enjoy your friendships more than you ever have? Be honest with yourself.

Jesus knew "the eyes of man are never satisfied" (Prov. 27:20). *Some things matter more than money.*

Jesus knew this.

Prayer

Father, as I achieve success, please remind me and give me the wisdom to know that money is not an ends, but a means. It cannot bring me happiness, but giving it to help others can. Thank You that many things matter more than money. In Jesus' Name.

JESUS KNEW THE POWER OF WORDS AND THE POWER OF SILENCE

"He that hath knowledge spareth his words: and a man of understanding is of an excellent spirit. Even a fool, when he holdeth his peace, is counted wise: and he that shutteth his lips is esteemed a man of understanding."

Proverbs 17:27,28

Words are not cheap.

Wars begin because of *words.* Peace comes when great men get together and negotiate and dialogue. *Words link people.* Words are the bridge into your future.

Words *created the world.* (Gen. 1:3-31.)

Words *create your world.* (Prov. 18:21.)

Jesus said that your words reveal what kind of heart you possess. "...For of the abundance of the heart his mouth speaketh" (Luke 6:45).

Jesus said words can move mountains. (Mark 11:23.)

There is a time to *talk.* There is a time to *listen.* There is a time for *movement.* There is a time for *staying still.* When people were hungry for knowledge, Jesus spoke and taught for hours. But, when He got to Pontius Pilate's hall where truth was ignored, He was silent.

Your *words* matter. Conversation matters. "But I say unto you, That every idle word that men shall speak, they shall give account thereof in the day of judgement. For by thy words thou shalt be justified, and by thy words thou shalt be condemned" (Matt. 12:36,37). Be silent about injustices to you. Be silent in discussing the weaknesses of others. Be silent in advertising your own mistakes.

> ### WISDOM PRINCIPLE
> Silence Cannot Be Misquoted.

Jesus knew when to talk and when to listen.

Prayer

Father, give me the understanding that my words are like money. Each one is to be accounted for and not spent unwisely. Teach me how to guard my tongue and open my ears to listen. In Jesus' Name, I thank You that I will know when to speak and when to listen.

Ingredient #5

Attend The Right Church Suitable For Your Family

MASTER SECRET 31

JESUS KNEW WHEN YOU WANTED SOMETHING YOU HAVE NEVER HAD, YOU HAVE TO DO SOMETHING YOU HAVE NEVER DONE

"Now the LORD had said unto Abram, Get thee out of thy country, and from thy kindred, and from thy father's house, unto a land that I will shew thee: And I will make of thee a great nation, and I will bless thee, and make thy name great; and thou shalt be a blessing."

Genesis 12:1,2

Everything is difficult at first.

When you were beginning to crawl, it was very difficult. When you took your first step, and fell — that was difficult.

Thousands will fail in life because they are unwilling to make changes. They refuse to change jobs, towns, or friendships. They stay in comfort zones. Yet, thousands of others move up the ladder of happiness because they are willing to go through a little discomfort to experience a new level in life.

103

Peter wanted to walk on water. Jesus saw his excitement. Then He gave a simple instruction for Peter to do something he had never done before. "And he said, 'Come.' And when Peter was come down out of the ship, he walked on the water, to go to Jesus" (Matt. 14:29).

Jesus always gave people something to do. And it was always something *they had never done before.* He knew that their obedience was the only proof of their faith in Him.

Listen to the instructions to the Israelites: march around the walls of Jericho seven days in a row, and then seven times on Sunday. (Josh. 6.)

WISDOM PRINCIPLE

When You Want Something
You Have Never Had,
You Have Got To Do Something
You Have Never Done.

Listen to the prophet's instructions to a leper: go dip in the Jordan River seven times. You will be healed on the seventh time. (2 Kings 5.)

Ruth left her home country of Moab to be with Naomi, she met Boaz who changed her life forever. (Book of Ruth.)

Elijah stretched the faith of the widow who was down to her last meal. Two pancakes before death, he motivated her to do something she had never done — sow her seed in expectation of a harvest during famine. She saw the miracle come to pass. (1 Kings 17.)

Jesus knew how to stretch people's faith. He motivated them. *He helped them do things they had never done before in order to create things they had never had.*

Jesus did new things.

Prayer

Father, help me to move out of my comfort zone and realize that in order to achieve something I have never had, I must do something I have never done before. In Jesus' Name.

JESUS PERMITTED OTHERS TO CORRECT THEIR MISTAKES

"...for I will forgive their iniquity, and I will remember their sin no more."
Jeremiah 31:34c

Everybody makes mistakes. Everybody.

Examine the biographies of multi-millionaires. Many have experienced bankruptcy several times. They simply discovered that failure is not fatal. *Failure is merely an opinion.*

Jesus never disconnected from those who made mistakes with their life.

One of His favorite disciples was Peter. Peter denied Him. Yet, he confessed his sin. Jesus forgave him. He became one of the greatest apostles in the history of the church.

David committed adultery with Bathsheba. God forgave him. Look at Samson. He fell into sexual temptation with Delilah. Yet, he is one of the champions of faith mentioned in Hebrews 11:32.

Learn to forgive *yourself.* Learn to forgive *others.* Everybody hurts somewhere. Their mistakes stay on their mind. *Give them another chance.*

WISDOM PRINCIPLE
All Men Fall.
The Great Ones Get Back Up.

Mistakes are correctable.

Jesus knew this.

Prayer

Father, just as You have forgiven me, place inside of me the responsibility to forgive myself and others. There has been only one perfect man, and others will also make mistakes. Teach me to give people another chance. In Jesus' Name.

JESUS KNEW HIS WORTH

"A man's gift maketh room for him, and bringeth him before great men."

Proverbs 18:16

Know your gift.

Many around you may never discover you. It is not really important that they do. *What is really important is that you discover yourself, your gifts, your talents.*

Popularity is when *other people* like you. Happiness is *when you like yourself.*

There is an interesting scenario when Jesus visited the home of Lazarus and his two sisters, Mary and Martha. Martha, busy with housework, was agitated with Mary who was simply sitting at the feet of Jesus listening to every word He said. When she complained, Jesus replied, "Mary hath chosen that good part" (Luke 10:42).

He knew His personal worth. He knew that His own words were life. He was incredibly self-confident and *expected to be treated well.*

He honored those who discerned His worth.

Jesus even reacted favorably to a woman who washed His feet. "... Seest thou this woman? I entered into thine house, thou gavest me no water for my feet: but she hath washed my feet with tears, and wiped them with the hairs of her head. Thou gavest me no kiss: but this woman since the time I came in hath not ceased to kiss my feet. My head with oil thou didst not anoint: but this woman hath anointed my feet with ointment'' (Luke 7:44-46).

```
┌──── WISDOM PRINCIPLE ────┐
│                          │
│    Happiness Is When You │
│      Like Yourself.      │
│                          │
└──────────────────────────┘
```

Jesus knew His worth.

Prayer

Father, You have created me. Your Word proclaims that You have created only creatures of glory. Teach me to accept and like myself. Happiness begins with liking who I am. In Jesus' Name.

JESUS NEVER TRIED TO SUCCEED ALONE

"For by wise counsel thou shalt make thy war: and in multitude of counsellors there is safety."

Proverbs 24:6

You need people.

You need God.

Everything you have came from God. Success is a collection of relationships. Without clients, a lawyer has no career. Without patients, a doctor has no future. Without a composer, a singer has nothing to say.

Your future is connected to people, so develop people skills.

He constantly talked to His Heavenly Father. He talked to His disciples. He talked to everybody. At twelve, He exchanged with the scribes and priests in the temple. He talked to tax collectors, fishermen, doctors, and lawyers. He said, "I can of mine own self do nothing" (John 5:30).

You need problem-solvers in your life.

You need a good banker, doctor, and a financial advisor. You need your family. You need a godly pastor. You need people.

WISDOM PRINCIPLE

Your Rewards in Life Are
Determined by the Problems You
Solve for Someone Else.

Listen to the inner voice of the Holy Spirit today. Obey every instruction.

Jesus did.

Prayer

Father, no man can do it without others. Please give me guidance and wisdom in knowing who I can turn to. I know that my life depends on other people and how I help them. In Jesus' Name.

JESUS KNEW THAT MONEY IS ANYWHERE YOU REALLY WANT IT TO BE

"The thoughts of the diligent tend only to plenteousness...."

Proverbs 21:5a

Money is everywhere.

Money is anything of value. Your *time* is money. Your knowledge is money. Your *skills, gifts* and *talents* are money.

Stop seeing money as merely something you carry around in your wallet. View money as *anything you possess that solves a problem for someone.*

Money is everywhere. Jesus knew that money even existed in the most unlikely places. Money is *anywhere* you really want it to be.

Colonel Sanders wanted it to be in *something he loved,* his unique fried chicken. Mohammed Ali found his financial success in boxing.

Peter was a fisherman. Tax money was needed. Jesus told him where money could be found. "... Lest we should offend them, go thou to the sea, and cast an hook, and take up the fish that first cometh up; and when thou hast opened his mouth, thou shalt find a piece of money: that take, and give unto them for me and thee" (Matt. 17:27).

WISDOM PRINCIPLE

Money Exists in the Most
Unlikely Places.
Look.

Do you love flowers and long to make your living owning a florist shop? That is where your money can be found.

Jesus knew that money existed *everywhere.*

Prayer

Lord, I know that You are not limited by the world's definition of money. Please teach me how I can turn what I desire to do or be into money. With Your help I can accomplish Your desires. In Jesus' Name.

JESUS SET
SPECIFIC GOALS

"The wisdom of the prudent is to understand his way...."

Proverbs 14:8a

Decide what you really want.

In 1952 a prominent university discovered that only three out of one hundred graduates had written down a clear list of goals. Ten years later, their follow-up study showed that three percent of the graduating class had accomplished more financially than the remaining ninety-seven percent of the class.

Those three percent were the *same graduates* who had *written down their goals.* "Write the vision, and make it plain upon tables, that he may run that readeth it" (Hab. 2:2).

When you decide exactly *"what"* you want, the *"how* to do it" will emerge.

Jesus knew His purpose and mission. "For the Son of man is come to seek and to save that which was lost" (Luke 19:10).

He knew the product He had to offer. "The thief cometh not, but for to steal, and to kill, and to destroy: I am come that they might have life, and that they might have it more abundantly" (John 10:10).

114

Jesus had a sense of destiny. He knew where He wanted to go. He knew where people needed Him. (John 4:3).

WISDOM PRINCIPLE

When You Decide What You Want, the "How-To-Do-It" Will Emerge.

Jesus knew that achievers were detail oriented. "For which of you, intending to build a tower, sitteth not down first, and counteth the cost, whether he have sufficient to finish it?" (Luke 14:28).

Take four sheets of paper. At the top of sheet number one, write, "My lifetime dreams and goals."

Now write in total detail everything you would like to become, do, or have during your lifetime. *Dream your dreams in detail on paper.*

Now, take sheet number two and write, "My twelve month goals."

Now list everything you want to get done within the next twelve months.

Now, take the third sheet of paper and write, "My thirty day goals."

Now write out in detail what you would like to accomplish for the next thirty days.

Now take the fourth sheet of paper and write, "My ideal success daily routine."

Now write down the six most important things you will do in the next twenty-four hours.

The secret of your future is hidden in your daily routine. Set your goals.

Jesus knew this.

Prayer

Father, You have placed within me the ability and desire to succeed. I will plan to succeed and will write down my plan for success. I ask for insight into Your plan for my life. In Jesus' Name.

Ingredient #6
Involve Quality People
In Your Life

JESUS KNEW THAT EVERY GREAT ACHIEVEMENT REQUIRED A WILLINGNESS TO BEGIN SMALL

"As for me, behold, my covenant is with thee, and thou shalt be a father of many nations. Neither shall thy name any more be called Abram, but thy name shall be Abraham; for a father of many nations have I made thee. And I will make thee exceeding fruitful, and I will make nations of thee, and kings shall come out of thee. And I will establish my covenant between me and thee and thy seed after thee in their generations for an everlasting covenant, to be a God unto thee, and to thy seed after thee."

Genesis 17:4-7

Everything big starts little.

Think for just a moment. An oak tree began as an acorn. A six foot man began as a small, small embryo in a mother's womb.

Be willing to begin small. *Start with whatever you have.* Everything you possess is a starting point. Do not be like the man in the Bible who had one talent and refused to use it. *Use whatever you have been given, and more will come to you.*

Jesus began in a stable. But He did not stay there. He went thirty years without performing miracles. But one day He launched His first miracle. The rest is history.

David had a slingshot. But he *became* a king.

Joseph was sold as a slave. But he *became* the Prime Minister of Egypt.

The widow of Zarephath had a small pancake. But she sowed it into the work of God and created a continuous supply during the famine.

Whatever you have been given is enough to create anything you have been promised.

> ── **WISDOM PRINCIPLE** ──
>
> Whatever You Have in Your
> Hand Can Create Anything You
> Want in Your Future

"For who hath despised the day of small things?" (Zech. 4:10). "For precept must be upon precept, precept upon precept; line upon line, line upon line; here a little, and there a little" (Isa. 28:10).

Whatever you possess today is enough to create anything else you will ever want in your future.

Jesus existed before the foundation of the world. He remembered when the earth and the human race did not even exist. That is why He did not mind the beginning in a stable.

Jesus knew *great things started small.*

Prayer

Father, I thank You that You have equipped me now with what I need to achieve success. I know that if I am willing to start small and serve others, You will honor me and elevate me to a higher position. In Jesus' Name.

MASTER SECRET 38

JESUS HURT WHEN OTHERS HURT

"Rejoice with them that do rejoice, and weep with them that weep."

Romans 12:15

Someone close to you is in trouble.

Have you really noticed it? Does it matter to you at all? Everybody hurts somewhere. *When others hurt, try to feel it.*

You are a solution to somebody with a problem. Find them. Listen for their cry.

You are their walking life jacket. You hold the key to their lock. Feel it.

Jesus did. Jesus did not hide in the palace. He was not a recluse. He walked where people walked. *He hurt when people hurt.*

"And Jesus went forth, and saw a great multitude, and was moved with compassion toward them, and he healed their sick" (Matt. 14:14).

Jesus feels what you feel. "For we have not an high priest which cannot be touched with the feeling of our infirmities; but was in all points tempted like as we are, yet without sin" (Heb. 4:15).

You will begin to succeed with your life when the hurt and problems of others begin to matter to you.

> ──── **WISDOM PRINCIPLE** ────
>
> The Broken Become Masters
> at Mending.

Several years ago, I was invited to attend a Christmas party for a large law firm here in Dallas. One of the young lawyers told an unforgettable story that night. He was the protege of one of the great lawyers in the midwest. This renowned lawyer won practically every case. In fact, every one of his settlements were million dollar settlements. The young lawyer simply could not figure it out. He said, ''The research was normal. The reading material seemed normal. The stack of information we had collected seemed average before he got in front of the jury.''

Then he said, ''This old lawyer would walk back and forth before the jury. As he talked, a transformation took place on the faces of the jury. When they came back, they always gave his client huge settlements.''

That night at the Christmas party, the young lawyer told us how he probed his mentor and said, ''You must tell me your secret. I watch you carefully. I've read your material. But, none of us in the firm can figure out why your juries returned with million dollar verdicts. It is a mystery we cannot unravel.''

The old lawyer said, ''I would like to tell you, but you really would not believe me if I did.''

The young lawyer probed him month after month. For a long time the older lawyer insisted, ''It really would not mean anything to you.''

Finally one day when the young protege was going to leave his firm to go to another city, the old mentor said, "Take a drive with me." They went to a grocery store. The old lawyer filled the back of his car with groceries and they began to drive out into the country. It had snowed. It was freezing and the icy weather was cutting. They finally drove up to a very modest, inexpensive farm house. The old mentor instructed the young lawyer to help him carry in the groceries. When they went inside the home, the young lawyer saw a little boy sitting on a sofa. He looked closer and noticed that the little boy had both of his legs cut off. It happened in a car accident. The old lawyer spoke to the family for a few moments and said, "Just thought I would bring a few groceries for you since I know how difficult it is for you to get out in this kind of weather."

As they were driving back to the city, the old lawyer looked at the young lawyer and said, "It is quite simple. My clients *really do matter to me. I believe* in their cases. I *believe* they deserve the highest settlements that can be given. When I stand before a jury, somehow *they feel that*. They come back with the verdicts I desire. *I feel what my clients feel. The* jury *feels* what I *feel*."

```
┌──── WISDOM PRINCIPLE ────┐
│    Those Who Unlock Your    │
│ Compassion Are Those to Whom │
│   You Have Been Assigned.   │
└─────────────────────────┘
```

Jesus hurt when others hurt.

Prayer

Father, please open my eyes to those around me who are hurting. Teach me that achievement and success include caring for those around me. Help me have compassion on the broken and wounded. In Jesus' Name.

JESUS WAS NOT AFRAID TO SHOW HIS FEELINGS

''...the righteous are bold as a lion.''
Proverbs 28:1b

Emotions dictate world events.

An angered world leader attacks another country. Angry airline employees have a picket line at airports. A mother whose child is killed by a drunk driver launches a national campaign. Thousands are rallying to stop the abortions of millions of babies.

Feelings do matter in life.

In business, feelings are contagious. When a salesman is excited over his product, the customer feels it, and is influenced by it.

Jesus was not afraid to express Himself.

When He was infuriated, others knew it. ''And the Jews' Passover was at hand, and Jesus went up to Jerusalem, And found in the temple those that sold oxen and sheep and doves...And when he had made a scourge of small cords, he drove them all out of the temple...and poured out the changers' money, and overthrew the tables'' (John 2:13-15).

He was deeply moved with compassion when He saw multitudes wandering aimlessly without direction. ''But when he saw the multitudes, he was moved with compassion on them, because they fainted, and were scattered abroad, as sheep having no shepherd'' (Matt. 9:36).

```
┌──────── WISDOM PRINCIPLE ────────┐
│                                  │
│     The Problem That Infuriates  │
│       You the Most, Is the       │
│      Problem God Has Assigned     │
│          You To Solve.            │
│                                  │
└──────────────────────────────────┘
```

The Bible even records that Jesus wept openly. ''And when he was come near, he beheld the city, and wept over it'' (Luke 19:41).

I am not speaking about an uncontrollable temper, neither am I referring to someone who sobs and breaks down every time a problem occurs in their life.

Rather, I'm asking that you notice that Jesus did not bottle up His emotions. He was not a robot. He was enthusiastic when He saw a demonstration of faith, He wept when He saw unbelief.

Peter, His disciple, was affected by it. The Apostle Paul was set on fire by it. They changed the course of history.

Be bold in expressing your opinions. Feel strongly about the things that matter in life. You can be a marvelous influence for good.

You will always be drawn to people who are expressive. Thousands scream at rock concerts, football games and world championship boxing matches.

Don't be a spectator of life. *Get in the arena.*

Jesus was.

Prayer

Lord, I know that passion and enthusiasm for life are keys to success. Help me to find and direct godly passion and enthusiasm into my life. Teach me to be bold in expressing my opinions and feelings. Train me to be a player in life, not a spectator. In Jesus' Name.

JESUS KNEW THE POWER OF HABIT

"Then said Jesus to those Jews which believed on him, If ye continue in my word, then are ye my disciples indeed."

John 8:31

Great men simply have great habits.

A well-known billionaire said, "I arrive at my office at 7:00 a.m. It is a habit." Recently a best-selling novelist who has sold over one million books said, "I get up at the same time every morning. I start writing at 8:00 A.M. and I quit at 4:00 each afternoon. I do it every day. It is a habit."

Habit is a gift from God. *It simply means anything you do twice becomes easier.* It is the Creator's key in helping you succeed.

Jesus stayed busy. He traveled. He prayed for the sick. He taught and ministered. He supervised His disciples. He spoke to large crowds.

However, He had an important custom and habit. "And he came to Nazareth, where he had been brought up: AND, AS HIS CUSTOM WAS, he went into the synagogue on the sabbath day, and stood up for to read" (Luke 4:16).

WISDOM PRINCIPLE

You Will Never Change Your
Life Until You Change
Something You Do Daily.

Daniel prayed three times a day. (Daniel 6:10.) The psalmist prayed seven times daily. (Ps. 119:164.) The disciples of Jesus met on the first day of each week. (Acts 20:7.)

Jesus knew *great men simply have great habits.*

Prayer

Father, teach me to develop good habits, habits that lead to success. Give me the perseverence to persist in forming a habit that You desire for me. In Jesus' Name.

JESUS FINISHED WHAT HE STARTED

"The desire accomplished is sweet to the soul...."

Proverbs 13:19a

Champions are finishers.

It is fun to be creative. It is exciting to always be giving birth to new ideas, thinking of new places to go or launching a new product. But real champions complete things. They are *follow through* people.

Jesus was thirty years old when He started His ministry. His ministry went for three and a half years. He did many miracles. He touched many lives. He electrified the world through twelve men.

But hidden in the thousands of Scriptures is a golden principle that revealed His power. It happened on the horrible day of His crucifixion. He was taunted by thousands. Spears pierced His side. Spikes were driven into His hands. Eight inches of thorns were crushed into His brow. Blood had dried on His hair. Four hundred soldiers left spittle running down His body.

That is when He uttered perhaps the greatest sentence ever uttered on earth: "It is finished" (John 19:30). The sins of man could be forgiven. He paid the price. The plan was complete. He was the lamb led to the slaughter.

He was the chief cornerstone. (Eph. 2:20.) *The Prince of Peace had come.* (Isa. 9:6.) Our great high priest, the Son of God, was our golden link to the God of heaven. (Heb. 4:14.)

WISDOM PRINCIPLE

Your Exit Will Be Remembered
Longer Than Your Entry.

Jesus was a finisher. He finished what He started. The bridge that linked man to God was complete. Man could approach God without fear.

The Apostle Paul was a finisher. (2 Tim. 4:7.)

Solomon, the wisest man that ever lived was a finisher. (1 Kings 6:14.)

One famous multi-millionaire said, "I will pay a great salary to anyone who can complete an instruction that I give to him."

Start completing *little things.* Write that "Thank You" note to your friend. Make those two telephone calls.

Get the spirit of a finisher. "He that endureth to the end shall be saved" (Matt. 10:22).

Jesus was a *Finisher.*

Prayer

Father, give me the spirit of a finisher. Place in me the will and desire to complete what I have started. Give me Your strength to continue. In Jesus' Name.

JESUS WAS KNOWLEDGEABLE OF SCRIPTURE

"Thy word is a lamp unto my feet, and a light unto my path."

Psalm 119:105

When God talks, the wise listen.

The greatest book on earth is the Bible. It has outsold every book. It is the Word of God.

It takes approximately 56 hours to read the Bible through completely. If you read 40 chapters a day, you will complete the Bible within 30 days. If you read nine chapters a day in the New Testament you will finish reading the New Testament within 30 days. You should read the Bible systematically. Regularly. Expectantly.

Read Luke 4. When satan presented his temptation to Christ, Jesus merely quoted Scriptures back to him as answers. *The Word of God is powerful.* "Thy word have I hid in mine heart, that I might not sin against thee" (Ps. 119:11).

The book of Proverbs has 31 chapters. Why not sit down today and start a magnificent new habit: reading this wisdom book completely through each month? Simply read chapter one on the first day of each month, chapter two on the second and so forth.

WISDOM PRINCIPLE

Faith Comes When You Hear
God Talk.

The Word of God will build your faith. "So then faith cometh by hearing, and hearing by the word of God" (Rom. 10:17). Faith comes when you *hear* God talk. Faith comes when you *speak* the Word of God.

The Word of God keeps you pure. "Wherewithal shall a young man cleanse his way? by taking heed thereto according to thy word" (Ps. 119:9).

Jesus knew the Word.

Prayer

Father, I know that the Bible is Your Word and it has been given to me. I thank You, Father, for putting in my hands the means by which I can increase my faith and keep my purity. I commit, today, to read the Word and study it as I would the most important book in my life. In Jesus' Name.

Ingredient #7
Invest In Yourself

JESUS NEVER HURRIED

"In your patience possess ye your souls."

Luke 21:19

Impatience is costly.

This is an impatient generation. Fast foods, microwave ovens, and crowded freeways reflect this philosophy.

Your greatest mistakes will happen because of impatience.

Most businesses that fail, do so because of lack of preparation and time. Great businesses do not happen overnight. Even this great country took years to become an independent nation.

Take time to grow into your business. Be deliberate with your projects. Become a "long-termer."

Life is a marathon, not a fifty-yard dash.

Champions pace themselves. They see the big picture.

Jesus refused to be rushed by the emergencies of others. There are no scriptures recorded that show where He was hurried or ever in an emergency.

When one of His close friends Lazarus was sick, word was sent to Jesus. Mary and Martha, the sisters of Lazarus, wanted Jesus TO HURRY and pray for his healing before he died. *Jesus kept His own agenda.* An unhurried and unrushed agenda. Lazarus died. Here is the story:

> "Now a certain man was sick, named Lazarus, of Bethany, the town of Mary and her sister Martha...whose brother Lazarus was sick. Therefore, his sisters sent unto him, saying, Lord, behold, he whom thou lovest is sick. When Jesus heard that, he said, This sickness is not unto death, but for the glory of God...
>
> "Now Jesus loved Martha, and her sister, and Lazarus. When he had heard therefore that he was sick, he abode two days still in the same place where he was.
>
> "Then said Martha unto Jesus, Lord, if thou hadst been here, my brother had not died.
>
> "Jesus said unto her, Thy brother shall rise again."
>
> "And when he thus had spoken, he cried with a loud voice, Lazarus, come forth.
>
> "And he that was dead came forth, bound hand and foot with graveclothes: and his face was bound about with a napkin. Jesus saith unto them, Loose him, and let him go."
> John 11:1-6,21,23,43,44

Decisiveness is powerful and magnetic, but Jesus never made decisions due to pressure tactics from others. Refuse to be intimidated by statements such as, "This is the last one available this year. If you don't buy it now, you may not get another chance."

WISDOM PRINCIPLE

Patience Is the Weapon
That Forces Deception
To Reveal Itself.

Skilled negotiators teach that *waiting is a weapon.* Whoever is the most hurried and impatient usually ends up with the worst end of the deal.

Take time to do things right. The weakness and flaws of any plan are often buried by flurry and hurry.

Jesus knew this.

Prayer

Father, give me patience. Teach me to wait until I hear from You and know that the time is right. Thank You for giving me patience and the desire to do things correctly. In Jesus' Name.

JESUS WENT WHERE HE WAS CELEBRATED INSTEAD OF WHERE HE WAS TOLERATED

"For better it is that it be said unto thee, Come up hither; than that thou shouldest be put lower in the presence of the prince whom thine eyes have seen."

Proverbs 25:7

Never stay where you are not valued.

Never stay where you have not been assigned. Treasure your gift. Guard well any talent God has given to you. Know this — God has prepared those to receive you when you are at the place of your assignment.

Jesus was unable to do any miracles in certain cities. The people doubted. Unbelief was like a cancer in the atmosphere. It stopped Him from releasing the healing flow.

He taught His disciples to disconnect from any place that did not see their worth. "And whosoever shall not receive you, nor hear your words, when ye depart out of that house or city, shake off the dust of your feet" (Matt. 10:14. See also Prov. 25:17.)

```
┌──── WISDOM PRINCIPLE ────┐
│  Never Expect a 16" x 20" Idea To Be  │
│   Celebrated by a 3" x 5" Mind.   │
└──────────────────────────┘
```

It is foolish to waste your entire life on those who do not celebrate you. *Move on.*

Jesus did.

Prayer

Lord, I ask that You give me the wisdom and discernment to stay where I am valued and leave the places that I am not valued. Teach me not to waste my life on foolish things. In Jesus' Name.

JESUS CONSTANTLY CONSULTED HIS HEAVENLY FATHER

"Where no counsel is, the people fall: but in the multitude of counsellors there is safety."

Proverbs 11:14

Learn to reach.

A famous billionaire of our day was trained by his father. In one of his recent books he said that he called his father a dozen times a week. He also telephones his own office ten to twelve times a day. He said, "If I don't constantly stay in touch with my business, it's gone." Stay in touch with your supervisor, your boss, *anyone who supervises you, mentors you or is guiding you into something you want to accomplish.* Stay in touch regularly.

Jesus was brilliant. He was a miracle worker. He *constantly consulted* His heavenly Father. "Then answered Jesus and said unto them, . . . Verily, verily, I say unto you, The Son can do nothing of himself, but what he seeth the Father do: for what things soever he doeth, these also doeth the Son likewise" (John 5:19).

Jesus was open to His Father about His feelings. In the garden of Gethsemane, He cried, " . . . O my Father, if it be possible, let this cup pass from me: nevertheless, not as I will, but as thou wilt" (Matt. 26:39).

Jesus was persistent in pursuing His father. "He went away again the second time, and prayed..." (Matt. 26:42). Jesus felt alone. He lived in our world. He felt the feelings you feel. He is our elder brother. *And, He was not too proud to reach.*

```
┌───────── WISDOM PRINCIPLE ─────────┐
│                                     │
│   Mentors Are Bridges to Tomorrow   │
│                                     │
└─────────────────────────────────────┘
```

Know the power of connection. Create contact. Know it's the first step toward increase. *Somebody is a link to your future successes.* Tomorrow hinges on your ability to pursue them. Do it.

Jesus reached.

Prayer

Father, give me the intelligence and humility to consult those who are guiding me. Put in me the desire to remain humble and seek after You every day. Father, please keep me from becoming too proud to reach. In Jesus' Name.

JESUS KNEW THAT PRAYER GENERATES RESULTS

"And in the morning, rising up a great while before day, he [Jesus] went out, and departed into a solitary place, and there prayed."

Mark 1:35

Prayer works.

Satan dreads your prayer link to God. He will attempt to sabotage it in any way possible. Don't let him. *Make a daily appointment with God.* You make appointments with your dentist. You make appointments with your lawyer. Schedule a specific moment with God.

You will never be the same.

Jesus prayed during crisis times. Just before His crucifixion, He prayed three different times to His Father. (Matt. 26:44.)

He taught His disciples how to pray. There are six important words to remember as you read "the Lord's Prayer." (Matt. 6:9.)

1) *Praise.* "...Our Father which art in heaven, Hallowed be thy name" (Matt. 6:9). Here is an important place to remember that God assigned Himself numerous names. Jehovah-Jirah which means "the Lord provideth." Jehovah-Raphe — "the Lord that heals."

2) *Priorities.* "Thy kingdom come. They will be done in earth, as it is in heaven" (Matt. 6:10). This is where you ask the Lord to implement His plan for each day. His will to be done in government, on your job, in your home, and in your personal life.

3) *Provision.* "Give us this day our daily bread" (Matt. 6:11). When you pray, begin to thank God that He is providing all the finances that you need for your life.

4) *Pardon.* "And forgive us our debts, as we forgive our debtors" (Matt. 6:12). Here, Jesus instructs His disciples to release forgiveness and pardon to those who have sinned against them. What you make happen for others, God will make happen for you. Mercy is given freely to those who *give it* freely.

5) *Protection.* "And lead us not into temptation, but deliver us from evil" (Matt. 6:13). Jesus taught His disciples here to pray for total protection throughout their day.

6) *Praise.* "For thine is the kingdom, and the power, and the glory, for ever. Amen" (Matt. 6:13). Jesus taught them to end this prayer time again with praise to their Heavenly Father for who He is and the power that He releases into their life.

> **WISDOM PRINCIPLE**
>
> When You Get in the Presence
> of God Your Best Ideas
> Will Surface.

Keep a prayer list. Set a special time each day, have a special place if possible.

Don't forget the *prayer of agreement;* "...If two of you shall agree on earth as touching any thing that they shall ask, it shall be done for them of my Father which is in heaven" (Matt. 18:19).

Jesus *prayed.*

Prayer

Father, thank You for prayer! I know that when I am in Your presence, You will reveal Your plans and desires to me. Constantly remind me that prayer works, and always will. In Jesus' Name.

JESUS ROSE EARLY

"Wherefore now rise up early in the morning with thy master's servants that are come with thee: and as soon as ye be up early in the morning, and have light, depart."

1 Samuel 29:10

Champions seize their day.

Famous successful men usually get up early. Get an early start every day. You will be amazed how much you can accomplish when others are just beginning their day.

Jesus rose early. "And in the morning, rising up a great while before day, he went out, and departed into a solitary place, and there prayed" (Mark 1:35). He consulted His Heavenly Father before He consulted anyone else. He pursued the influence of God — early.

Joshua rose early. (Josh. 6:12.)

Moses, the great deliverer of the Israelites, rose early. (Ex. 8:20.) Abraham, the great Patriarch of the Jewish nation rose early. (Gen. 19:27.)

You think more clearly in the morning. You can *focus.* Your day is *uncluttered.* As you accumulate the emotions and stress of others throughout the day, the quality of your work usually deteriorates.

145

WISDOM PRINCIPLE

He Who Masters His Time,
Masters His Life.

Your life style may be an exception to this rule. Many people work all night, and use their day time for sleeping. But, for the most part, most of us have discovered that the greatest hours of your day are early, uncluttered with the demands of others.

Jesus knew this.

Prayer

Lord, teach me to seize the day. Give me the knowledge to master my time, so that I can master my life. You have given me gifts and talents that I cannot waste in sleep. Motivate me and prompt me. In Jesus' Name.

JESUS NEVER FELT HE HAD TO PROVE HIMSELF TO ANYONE

"Give not that which is holy unto the dogs, neither cast ye your pearls before swine, lest they trample them under their feet, and turn again and rend you."

Matthew 7:6

You are already important.

You have nothing to prove to anyone. You are the offspring of a remarkable Creator. You have the mind of Christ. Your gifts and talents have been placed within you. *Find what they are. Celebrate them.* Find ways to use those gifts to improve others and help them achieve their dreams and goals.

But never, never, never exhaust and waste your energies trying to prove something to somebody else.

Worth must be discerned.

Jesus knew this. Satan tempted Him. "...If thou be the son of God, command that these stones be made bread (Matt. 4:3).

Jesus unstopped deaf ears. He opened blind eyes. He made the lame to walk. The dead were raised. Sinners were changed. Yet, the jeers of the doubters continued to scream into His ears at His crucifixion,

147

"And saying, Thou that destroyeth the temple, and buildest it in three days, save thyself. If thou be the Son of God, come down from the cross" (Matt. 27:40).

```
┌─────── WISDOM PRINCIPLE ───────┐
│                                │
│     Those Who Do Not Discern   │
│     Your Worth Are Disqualified│
│        For Relationship.       │
│                                │
└────────────────────────────────┘
```

What was Jesus' reaction? *He was confident of His worth.* He knew His *purpose. He refused to let the taunts of ignorant men change His plans.*

You are not responsible for anything but an honest effort to please God. *Keep focused.*

Jesus did.

Prayer

Father, I thank You for not making me responsible for anything but an honest effort to please You. Help me to remember that I do not find my value in what others think of me, but in what You think of me. In Jesus' Name.

Ingredient #8
Value and
Discipline Time

JESUS AVOIDED UNNECESSARY CONFRONTATIONS

"Recompense to no man evil for evil. Provide things honest in the sight of all men. If is be possible, as much as lieth in you, live peaceably with all men. Dearly beloved, avenge not yourselves, but rather give place unto wrath: for it is written, Vengeance is mine; I will repay, saith the Lord."

Romans 12:17-19

Stay away from unnecessary conflict.

It is exhausting. It is unproductive. Quarrelling and arguing are a waste of time. Millions of dollars have been lost in negotiations because of an argumentative spirit. Warfare is costly. And nobody really wins.

Jesus knew the emptiness of anger. "And all they in the synagogue, when they heard these things, were filled with wrath, And rose up, and thrust him out of the city, and led him unto the brow of the hill whereon their city was built, that they might cast him down headlong. But he passing through the midst of them went his way" (Luke 4:28-30).

He went His way.

He did not oppose them. He did not fight them. *He had other plans.* He was about His Father's business. He *focused on His own goals.* "And came down to Capernaum, a city of Galilee, and taught them on the sabbath days" (Luke 4:31).

He did not withdraw into depression. He did not enter into an unnecessary dialogue with them. He didn't cower in a corner of His parent's home. *He proceeds toward His mission and purpose.*

WISDOM PRINCIPLE

The Atmosphere You Permit Decides the Product You Produce.

Learn to keep your mouth shut. "Whoso keepeth his mouth and his tongue keepeth his soul from troubles" (Prov. 21:23).

Jesus was a peacemaker.

Prayer

Father, help me keep my mouth shut and stay in an atmosphere of peace and productivity. Do not let me wander down the path of quarreling and confusion. Keep me focused on the task at hand. In Jesus' Name.

| MASTER | |
| SECRET | 50 |

JESUS DELEGATED

"And in those days, when the number of the disciples was multiplied, there arose a murmuring of the Grecians against the Hebrews, because their widows were neglected in the daily ministration. Then the twelve called the multitude of the disciples unto them, and said, It is not reason that we should leave the word of God, and serve tables. Wherefore, brethren, look ye out among you seven men of honest report, full of the Holy Ghost and wisdom, whom we may appoint over this business. But we will give ourselves continually to prayer, and to the ministry of the word."

Acts 6:1-4

Know your limitations.

It is more productive to get ten men to work rather than you do the work of ten men. *Delegation is simply giving others necessary instructions and motivation to complete a particular task.* This takes time. It takes patience. But it is a long-term benefit.

He commanded the multitudes. He instructed His disciples to have the people sit down. He distributed the loaves and fishes to His disciples for distribution. (Matt. 14:19.) He sent His disciples to get a donkey. (Matt. 21:2.) He gave instructions to a blind man to complete his healing. (John 9:6,7.) He sent His disciples into cities to prepare for special meals. (Mark 14:12-15.)

There are some important things you need to remember when you network with others:

1. Make a checklist of their exact responsibilities.

2. Carefully instruct them as to your exact expectations of them.

3. Give them the information and authority necessary to complete those tasks.

4. Set a specific deadline to finish the task.

5. Clearly show them how they will be rewarded for their effort.

WISDOM PRINCIPLE

One Cannot Multiply.

Make the time to motivate and educate them as to your exact expectations. *Take the time to delegate.*

Jesus did.

Prayer

Lord, place in me the wisdom and responsibility to delegate. Teach me trust in others and the meaning of realistic expectations. Thank You that You have given me a successful example of delegation through Your Son. In Jesus' Name.

JESUS CAREFULLY GUARDED HIS PERSONAL SCHEDULE

"...a wise man's heart discerneth both time and judgment."

Ecclesiastes 8:5b

Your daily agenda is your life.

You cannot save time. You cannot collect it. You cannot place it in a special bank vault. You are only permitted to *spend* it, wisely or foolishly. *You must do something with time.*

You will invest it or you will waste it.

Everyone has a hidden agenda. Those around you will be reaching to pull you "off course." You must be careful to *protect your list of priorities.*

Jesus did. There is a fascinating story in the Bible about it.

Lazarus, a close friend of Jesus, became sick. Mary and Martha, His two sisters sent word to Jesus to come. However, "When he had heard therefore that he was sick, he abode two days still in the same place where he was" (John 11:6). Mary was upset, "Lord, if thou hadst been here, my brother had not died" (John 11:21).

But Jesus had deliberately delayed His coming. He kept His own schedule. He protected His agenda. He did not allow emergencies of others to get Him off track. *He guarded His list of priorities.*

WISDOM PRINCIPLE

Only You Know Your Priorities.

Make today count. Remember the 24 golden box cars on the track of success. *If you do not control what goes into each of your 24 golden box cars (hours), then somebody else will.*

Avoid distractions. Write your daily list of things to do. Protect your schedule. *This is your life.* Make it happen.

Jesus did.

Prayer

Father, give me the discretion and strength to protect my schedule. Teach me how to organize my time and give proper place to my priorities. In Jesus' Name.

JESUS ASKED QUESTIONS TO ACCURATELY DETERMINE THE NEEDS AND DESIRES OF OTHERS

"Hear counsel, and receive instruction, that thou mayest be wise in thy latter end."
Proverbs 19:20

Ask questions.

Interrogate your world. Insist on listening to the opinions and needs of others.

Almost nobody on earth listens to others, nor questions them.

It is a master secret of success.

Jesus asked questions.

Once Simon Peter went fishing. He caught nothing. When the morning was come, Jesus was standing on the shore. Jesus calls out, "Children, have ye any meat?..." (John 21:5). *He assumed nothing. He pursued information.*

Their answer was His entry point into their life. He had something they needed. *He had information.*

His question was a link to their future. *It was the bridge for their relationship.* He then instructed them,

"Cast the net on the right side of the ship, and ye shall find..." (John 21:6).

```
┌──── WISDOM PRINCIPLE ────┐
│   Information Is the Difference   │
│   Between Your Present and   │
│   Your Future.   │
└──────────────────────┘
```

Document the needs of others. Keep a Rolodex. Keep a notebook of their needs and desires. What are your customers' needs today? Are you *really listening* to them? Do they really feel you are listening to them? Most employees feel that their bosses really do not hear their complaints. Most employers feel that their employees do not interpret them correctly.

Jesus pursued information.

Prayer

Father, open my eyes and ears to correctly see and hear information. Constantly remind me of the importance of information and how it can determine my success. In Jesus' Name.

JESUS ALWAYS ANSWERED TRUTHFULLY

''...He that sweareth to his own hurt, and changeth not.''

Psalm 15:4b

Be truthful.

Someone has said, ''Tell the truth the first time, and you will never have to try and remember what you said.'' Truth will always outlast the storms of slander and false accusations.

Never misrepresent your product to a customer.

Carefully build and forge before your family the picture of total truth.

Nothing is more important in life than believability. When you lose that, you have lost the essence of favor, love, and success.

Jesus was Truth.

''...I am the way, the truth, and the life: no man cometh unto the Father, but by me'' (John 14:6). His integrity intimidated hypocrites. They reacted to His purity. Honesty is a force. It will destroy mountains of prejudice and fear in a single blow. ''God is not a man, that he should lie; neither the son of man, that he should repent: hath he said, and shall he not do

it? or hath he spoken, and shall he not make it good?''
(Num. 23:19).

```
┌─────── WISDOM PRINCIPLE ───────┐
│                                 │
│    Truth Is the Most Powerful   │
│    Force on Earth Because       │
│    It Cannot Be Changed.        │
│                                 │
└─────────────────────────────────┘
```

Jesus was *always* truthful.

Prayer

Father, teach me to guard my mouth and let only truth come out of it. Since truth cannot be changed, truth that I speak can change the world. In Jesus' Name.

JESUS STAYED IN THE CENTER OF HIS EXPERTISE

"And also that every man should eat and drink, and enjoy the good of all his labour, it is the gift of God."

Ecclesiastes 3:13

Do what you do best.

What do you *love* to do? What do you *love* to talk about? What would you rather *hear* about than anything else on earth? What would you do with your life *if money was not a factor?* What do you do *best* of all?

Your joy is determined by doing what you love.

Jesus associated with fishermen. He talked to tax collectors. Doctors and lawyers and religious leaders were regularly in His life. *But He never wavered from His focus.* "How God anointed Jesus of Nazareth with the Holy Ghost and with power: who went about doing good, and healing all that were oppressed of the devil; for God was with him" (Acts 10:38).

He knew His mission.

He stayed focused. I really believe that *broken focus is the real reason men fail.*

160

> ## ┌─ WISDOM PRINCIPLE ─┐
> The Only Reason Men Fail Is
> Broken Focus.

Some people take jobs because they are convenient or close to their home. One man told me that he had spent his entire life working on a job that made him miserable.

"Why have you worked there for twenty-seven years then?" I asked.

"It's only ten minutes from my house," he replied. "And in three years I will receive a gold watch. I don't want to leave too early and miss my gold watch."

What you love is a clue to your calling and talent.

Jesus knew this.

Prayer

Father, You have placed within me a specific design and purpose. Teach me to always stay on this focus and perform with excellence the talents You have given me. In Jesus' Name.

Ingredient #9
Discover and Develop
Your Own Talents

JESUS ACCEPTED THE RESPONSIBILITY FOR THE MISTAKES OF THOSE UNDER HIS AUTHORITY

"And be ye kind one to another, tenderhearted, forgiving one another, even as God for Christ's sake hath forgiven you."

Ephesians 4:32

People make mistakes.

This is not a perfect world. Your business is not a perfect business. Your friendships are not flawless. Those who work with you will make errors.

Remember, *you are mentoring those who receive your instructions.* They are in a process of growing. They are learning. They will stumble and make mistakes. Some of them will be costly.

I read an interesting story some years ago. An executive secretary to the president of a large corporation made a costly mistake. It cost the company $50,000.00. She was devastated and brought her letter of resignation to the president explaining, "I realize what a dumb thing I did. I am very sorry. I know that it cost the company $50,000.00. Here is my letter of resignation."

"Are you crazy?" he thundered. "I have been teaching you and educating you every week. Now, you have made a big mistake. I have just invested $50,000.00 in your education and you're going to leave? No, ma'am. You are not going to leave. You have cost me too much to lose my investment in you." She stayed and became an extraordinary executive.

```
┌──── WISDOM PRINCIPLE ────┐
│                          │
│     Forgiveness Makes a  │
│     Future Possible.     │
│                          │
└──────────────────────────┘
```

Peter denied the Lord. And yet Jesus lovingly said, "Simon, Simon, behold, Satan hath desired to have you, that he may sift you as wheat: but I have prayed for thee, that thy faith fail not: and when thou art converted, strengthen thy brethren" (Luke 22:31,32).

Great leaders accept the responsibility for their troops. If you are going to have extraordinary success in your business, be strong and courageous enough to take the responsibility for the mistakes of those in the process of learning from you. Don't whine. Don't complain. Be strong.

Jesus was our supreme example.

Prayer

Father, teach me to forgive and always remind me that no man or woman is perfect. Give me the courage and foresight to accept responsibility for those for whom I am responsible. Teach me to follow in the footsteps of Jesus. In Jesus' Name.

JESUS PURSUED THE MENTORSHIP OF MORE EXPERIENCED MEN

"Ointment and perfume rejoice the heart: so doth the sweetness of a man's friend by hearty counsel."

Proverbs 27:9

Mentors are teachers in your life.

Your mentors are not perfect people. They simply have experienced life and are capable of transferring that knowledge into you. Your mentor can be older or younger than yourself. Your mentor is *anyone capable of growing and increasing your life.*

Show me your mentors, and I can predict your future. "A wise man will hear, and will increase learning; and a man of understanding shall attain unto wise counsels" (Prov. 1:5).

Jesus sought knowledge. When He was twelve, He pursued the teachers of His day. "And it came to pass, that after three days they found him in the temple, sitting in the midst of the doctors, both hearing them, and asking them questions" (Luke 2:46).

Ruth listened to the advice of Naomi. Esther listened to Mordecai. David sat at the feet of Samuel. Joshua received instructions from Moses. Timothy was mentored by Paul. Elisha ran to stay in the presence of Elijah.

WISDOM PRINCIPLE
Know Greatness When
You Get in the Presence of It.

"And when they saw him, they were amazed: and his mother said unto him, Son, why hast thou thus dealt with us? behold, thy father and I have sought thee sorrowing. And He said unto them, How is it ye sought me? wist ye not that I must be about my Father's business?" (Luke 2:48,49).

Solomon said, "Where no counsel is, the people fall: but in the multitude of counsellors there is safety" (Prov. 11:14). "He that walketh with wise men shall be wise: but a companion of fools shall be destroyed" (Prov. 13:20).

Listen to your mentors. Sit in their presence. Purchase their tapes. Absorb their books. *One sentence can be the golden door to the next season of your life.*

WISDOM PRINCIPLE
The First Step Toward Success Is
the Willingness To Listen.

Jesus was teachable.

Prayer
Father, give me the humility and willingness to listen. Thank You for giving me the discernment to know when I should open my ears, and when I should not. You have given me the opportunity to learn and achieve. In Jesus' Name.

JESUS DID NOT PERMIT THOSE HE LED TO SHOW DISRESPECT

"For where envying and strife is, there is confusion and every evil work."

James 3:16

Never tolerate strife.

Strife will not go away voluntarily. You must confront it. *You will never correct what you are unwilling to confront.* Always name rebellion for what it is. Pinpoint rebellion. When there is a rebel in your company, discern it. *Mark those who create strife.* "Now I beseech you, brethren, mark them which cause divisions and offences contrary to the doctrine which ye have learned; and avoid them" (Rom. 16:17).

Jesus loved people. He cherished hours with His disciples. He was a listener. He was gracious and humble. But, He was quite aware of something that every successful person should remember: *familiarity can often incubate disrespect.*

One day Peter began to feel extra comfortable with Jesus. Comfortable enough to correct Him. "Then Peter took him, and began to rebuke him, saying, Be it far from thee, Lord: this shall not be unto thee" (Matt. 16:22).

Suddenly, the gentle and kind Jesus revealed His nature of steel. He was immovable. He was unshakable. And in a single stroke of communication, He stripped Peter of his cockiness. Peter had *presumed* on the relationship. Jesus had *never* given him the authority to correct Him. "But He turned, and said unto Peter, 'Get thee behind me, Satan: thou art an offence unto me: for thou savourest not the things that be of God, but those that be of men." (Matt. 16:23).

┌─── **WISDOM PRINCIPLE** ───┐

Never Complain About What
You Permit.

└─────────────────────────┘

Jesus did not tolerate disrespect.

You see, rebellion is contagious. One rebel can destroy thousands of people. *Confront those who cause contention.* Do not expect them to fade into the sunset. They never do.

Your business success depends on a peaceful and happy climate. You must constantly be aware of signs of discontent. Deal with it before it spreads like a virus throughout your organization.

One of the famous staff managers for a United States President says, "I manage by the acorn management philosophy. I look for problems when they are the size of an acorn. I refuse to watch them grow into oak trees."

People rarely respect and follow anyone they are capable of intimidating, dominating or manipulating.

Jesus knew this.

Prayer

Lord, grant me the discernment and courage to keep those under my authority from being disrespectful. Teach me how to respond to them in a manner that will defuse the wrong attitudes and guide them towards higher standards. In Jesus' Name.

JESUS UNDERSTOOD
SEED-FAITH

"Be not deceived; God is not mocked: for whatsoever a man soweth, that shall he also reap."

Galatians 6:7

Everything begins with a seed.

Someone plants a small acorn. It becomes the mighty oak tree. The small kernel of corn is planted. It produces two cornstalks. Each stalk produces two ears of corn. Each ear of corn contains over seven hundred kernels of corn. From that one small kernel of corn, a seed, 2,800 more kernels are created.

Look at *seed as anything that can multiply and become more.* Love is a seed. Money is a seed. Everything you possess can be planted back into the world as a *seed.*

Your seed is anything that benefits another person.

Your harvest is anything that benefits you.

Seed-Faith simply means to plant *something you have,* like a seed, in faith, *for a specific harvest.*

Seed-Faith is using what you have been given, to create something else you have been promised. If you sow the seed of diligence on your job, your harvest will be a promotion. "The soul of the sluggard desireth, and hath nothing: but the soul of the diligent shall be made fat" (Prov. 13:4). "He becometh poor that dealeth with a slack hand: but the hand of the diligent maketh rich" (Prov. 10:4).

When you sow love into your family, you will reap love. When you sow finances into the work of God, you will reap financial blessings.

```
┌──────── WISDOM PRINCIPLE ────────┐
│                                  │
│         Seed-Faith Is Using      │
│         What You Have To         │
│       Create What You Want.      │
│                                  │
└──────────────────────────────────┘
```

Jesus taught that giving was the beginning of blessings. "Give, and it shall be given unto you; good measure, pressed down, and shaken together, and running over, shall men give into your bosom. For with the same measure that ye mete withal it shall be measured to you again" (Luke 6:38).

This same scripture illustrates another incredible principle: *Whatever you are, you will create around you.* I am Irish. What will I create? Irishmen. What will a German create? Germans. What will a watermelon create? Watermelons. When you give, people around you start wanting to give to you.

It is simple, explosive and undeniable.

```
┌──────── WISDOM PRINCIPLE ────────┐
│                                  │
│       Giving Is the Only Proof   │
│      You Have Conquered Greed.   │
│                                  │
└──────────────────────────────────┘
```

Jesus taught the 100-fold principle. "And Jesus answered and said, Verily I say unto you, There is no man that hath left house, or brethren, or sisters, or father, or mother, or wife, or children, or lands, for my sake, and the gospel's, But he shall receive an hundredfold now in this time, houses, and brethren, and sisters, and mothers, and children, and lands, with persecutions; and in the world to come eternal life" (Mark 10:29,30).

Everything you have came from God. *Everything you will receive* in your future will come from God. He is your total Source for everything in your life. Never forget this.

He wants you to have His blessings. "For the Lord God is a sun and shield: the Lord will give grace and glory: no good thing will he withhold from them that walk uprightly" (Ps. 84:11). "Beloved, I wish above all things that thou mayest prosper and be in health, even as thy soul prospereth" (3 John 2).

WISDOM PRINCIPLE

When You Let Go of What Is
in Your Hand, God Will Let Go of
What Is in His Hand for You.

The secret of your future is determined by the seeds you sow today.

When you open your heart, God will open His windows. Never forget that ten-percent of your income is holy seed. It is called *"The Tithe."* "Bring ye all the tithes into the storehouse, that there may be meat in mine house, and prove me now herewith, saith the Lord of hosts, if I will not open you the windows of heaven, and pour you out a blessing, that there shall not be room enough to receive it. And I will rebuke the devourer for your sakes, and he shall not destroy the fruits of your ground..." (Mal. 3:10,11).

You can give your way out of trouble. Your seed can create any future you want. Remember, God has a Son, Jesus. He *sowed* Him in the earth, to *produce* a family. *Millions are born again because of His best Seed.*

Jesus knew this.

Prayer

Father, thank You for seed-faith. I am joyful that I receive what I give. That if I plant good seed, I will reap good seed. Lord, keep this principle always before me and teach me to honor it always. In Jesus' Name.

THE GRASSHOPPER COMPLEX

''Wherefore thou art no more a servant, but a son; and if a son, then an heir of God through Christ.''

Galatians 4:7

A few years ago, God gave me one of the most explosive concepts I've ever received.

The story is found in the book of Numbers. Moses was leader of the Israelites. They had left Egypt (Failure Zone) and headed for their Canaan (Success Zone). Canaan was not a type of Heaven — it had giants, and Heaven contains no possible conflict.

Canaan is a symbol for our dreams, our goals, our places of victories. It is ''Success Territory.'' Every man should have goals of some sort. God intended for us to have them.

Abraham's dream was a son, Isaac. Joseph had a dream: to be prime minister. Solomon wanted to build the temple. The Israelites had the promise of Canaan.

Moses sent twelve spies, or scouts, to review the land before entering. The men saw the land, rich in honey, milk, grapes . . . and *giants*. When they came back, their reports were contradictory. Ten men had evil reports, two had good reports. Ignoring the giants

174

was not what made their reports good or evil. All twelve recognized the existence of giants, even the two faith spies Joshua and Caleb. *Faith living is not ignoring the obvious.* Some people think if you recognize a problem situation, you are admitting doubt. That is incorrect.

Paul admitted once that Satan hindered him. (1 Thess. 2:18.) Peter spoke of an adversary. (1 Pet. 5:8.) Jesus, in Matthew 4, did not act as if Satan didn't exist.

Ignoring a cancer or financial bondage or a marriage problem doesn't dissolve it. *You must admit something exists before you can confront it successfully.* The sinner is never converted until he admits his need. The Baptism of the Holy Spirit comes only to those who realize they are "empty."

All twelve spies had faith.

The difference was — ten had faith in the *giants* — two had faith in *God.*

Ten were giant-conscious and two were *God-conscious.* Ten came back moaning, "Did you see the size of those GIANTS?" Joshua and Caleb came back licking their lips, saying, "Did you see the size of those GRAPES?" Ten were "*grasshoppers.*" Two were "giant-killers" and "grape-tasters!"

WISDOM PRINCIPLE

You Will Never Reach
the Palace Talking
Like a Peasant.

Your *conversation* reveals whether you are a winner or a loser. Losers major on their problems. Winners talk about the *possibilities*. Losers discuss their obstacles. Winners talk *opportunities*.

Losers talk disease. Winners talk about *health*. Losers talk about the devil's achievements. Winners talk about *God's victories*. Losers talk like victims. Winners talk like *victors*. Losers have a slaveship mentality. Winners have a *Sonship mentality*.

The Bible is a book of pictures. It gives you a picture of God, a picture of the devil, and God's photograph of YOU. You will accept one of three possible evaluations of your life.

1. What *you* think about yourself.

2. What *Satan* thinks about you.

3. What GOD thinks about you.

The ten spies said, "In our opinion, we are like grasshoppers. Even the giants think we are like grasshoppers."

I've heard many people talk as if they belonged to the First Church of the Grasshopper: "I'm nothing. I'm unworthy." A woman came up to me some time back saying, "Mike, I'm just nothing. I'm so unworthy."

I asked, "Did God create you?"

"Oh yes," she said.

I asked, "Do you think He puts trash together?"

She got the point.

God doesn't create cheap merchandise. YOU ARE HIS CREATION. YOU HAVE WORTH. YOU HAVE VALUE. HE IMPLANTED IN YOU THE SEEDS OF SUCCESS, FAITH AND

POWER. ACT LIKE IT. LIVE LIKE IT. Quit belittling yourself. Quit saying "I'm stupid, I'm dumb." *Do you have the mind of Christ?* Then you are super-brilliant! Say aloud, "I have the mind of Christ. I am amazed at the brilliant mind now in operation in my life." YOU ARE NO GRASSHOPPER! QUIT TALKING LIKE ONE! QUIT LIVING LIKE ONE!

Some weeks back, in the midst of a traumatic situation, I began to weep before God. For three hours I sobbed as if my heart would break. Suddenly, the Holy Spirit said, "SHUT UP!" (Have you ever had God talk like that to you? It is a bit strong! Even for this Irish lad.)

I said, "But God, I'm weeping over what I've lost in my life."

He said, "GET YOUR MIND OFF WHAT YOU DON'T HAVE. GET IT ON WHAT YOU DO HAVE."

Something exploded in my system. I had my mind on what I lacked instead of what I already possessed! There is a time to reach for that which you do not have — for that which seems impossible. THEN, THERE IS A TIME TO SIT BACK AND *CREATE A POWER CLIMATE OF THANKSGIVING FOR WHAT YOU POSSESS NOW!* Quit magnifying your problems. Quit exaggerating the power of the devil. Start emphasizing the power of your *God!* Start bragging about what God is planning for you TODAY! Start planning tomorrow's victories!

THE GRASSHOPPER COMPLEX will destroy your faith. It will stop the faith flow. It will give Satan a handle on your life. GET THE GIANT-KILLER INSTINCT. YOU ARE GREATER THAN THE ENEMY BECAUSE YOU ARE A "GOD-HOUSE." HE LIVES INSIDE YOU. Quit looking at the failure photographs Satan shows you of your yesterdays. God is keeping a photograph album of your victories, your future, your tomorrows! *God is not looking at where you stumbled yesterday, but at your possibilities tomorrow.*

THE GRASSHOPPER COMPLEX is what is destroying the power of the local church today.

It is paralyzing the faith flow. It is stopping the praise climate that God intended for us to create in the midst of our homes and our surroundings.

We talk like complainers instead of conquerors. WE ARE NOT GRASSHOPPERS. The ten spies talked about the size of the giants — but Joshua and Caleb talked about the size of the grapes!

Major on the opportunities, not the obstacles. *Start praising God* for what you already have — not just what you intend to have! If you are always reaching for that which is beyond your present possession, you will miss out on the joy of the "now" happiness — the "now" victory!

You can tell a GRASSHOPPER by his reaction to the greeting, "How are you?" He goes into the detailed "pain and hurt" routine. He talks about his health (or I should say his hurt, because few people go about telling how great their ears are hearing, their nose is smelling, their stomach is digesting, their eyes are seeing. They emphasize what is WRONG instead of what is RIGHT).

Grasshoppers love to talk about the *injustices of people* toward them, how they have been mistreated, and how people do not understand them. Have you ever heard a grasshopper stand before a group and say, "I give all the credit to being a failure to myself"? Absolutely not! They have a list of people who caused them to be what they are. (I think I may have a few grasshopper tendencies. Do you?)

Grasshoppers justify their lack of victory. They always give excuses for not conquering the devil. In fact, they sometimes even put down others who are walking and living victoriously.

Grasshoppers constantly talk about their *lack of finances.* Giant-killers talk about their *expectation* of God's provision.

Grasshoppers refer to their children's ages as the ''terrible twos.'' Giant-killers call that age the ''tremendous twos!''

I'm not saying it is easy. But to enjoy life, you must transfer from the GRASSHOPPER COMPLEX to the *GIANT-KILLER MENTALITY.*

It means you will have to *make up your mind to change.* You can CHANGE. God has given you the *power of choice:* the power to direct your thinking; your actions! Make up your mind to *destroy* the ''grasshopper complex.''

REINFORCE the giant-killer mentality by choosing FRIENDSHIPS that BUILD the faith life in *you.* You see, if you tolerate any other relationship it can be damaging to your spiritual growth.

GET CHOOSY. GET SELECTIVE. *Become more particular* in the friendships you allow.

Discipline your *music,* your *television viewing,* your *reading material.* Use material that will build up your self-confidence as well as your dependency on the Lord and the life of the Spirit.

Dare to become assertive in spiritual things. Dare to step out in faith. Dare to believe God for a new

MENTALITY. Dare to be positive about life. Dare to step UP . . . UP . . . UP . . . TO A POWER LIFE IN GOD.

ENTER THE WINNER'S WORLD!

Prayer

Father, thank You for creating me to succeed and not fail. Thank You that when I have faith in You and set my eyes upon Your will, I cannot fail. Keep me from falling into the grasshopper complex and lift me into the giant killer mentality. In Jesus' Name.

BORN TO TASTE
THE GRAPES*

"Blessed be the God and Father of our Lord Jesus Christ, who hath blessed us with all spiritual blessings in heavenly places in Christ."

Ephesians 1:3

Man is born with a need to *win* — *to conquer.*

Slavery is *unnatural.* Our mind functions from the view of the predator, not the prey. We are built to *dominate* the works of God's hands. Thus, the lion and elephant are in the cage and man became their keeper.

"Be fruitful, and multiply, and replenish the earth, and subdue it: and have dominion over the fish of the sea, and over the fowl of the air, and over every living thing that moveth upon the earth."

Genesis 1:28

Man craves *greatness.* We possess an obsession to expand, grow and improve. We were born for the "high place." We instinctively gravitate toward *increase:* spiritually, mentally and financially.

The *"seed of need"* was planted by the Creator. God made Himself a *necessity* for human happiness. Like

---

*This devotional, though longer than the others, contains valuable information and is well worth reading!

the missing puzzle piece, the life-picture doesn't make sense until He is included. We were built for *connection*. The *ear* demands *sounds*, the *eye* demands *sights*, the *mind* wants *negotiation*, the *heart* seeks *companionship*.

The God-connection is the bridge from failure to success.

Popularity is not success. Popularity is people liking you. Happiness is *you* liking *you*.

What Is Success?

Success is happiness. Happiness is feeling good about yourself. It is not necessarily fame, money or position. It is knowledge and awareness of your worth *in the eyes of God.*

You are here on purpose, designed and equipped for a *particular* function. You must discern and develop the God-given abilities He invested at your birth. *It is only when those gifts are being used properly that you will feel and know the value God sees in you.*

ELEVEN BENEFITS FROM GOD

The Book of Ephesians tells us the *respect and tenderness* in which God views us as His children.

1. He has *blessed* us. (1:3.)
2. He has *chosen* us. (1:4.)
3. He has *predestinated* us. (1:5.)
4. He has *accepted* us. (1:6.)
5. He has *redeemed* us. (1:7.)
6. He has *forgiven* us. (1:7.)
7. He has *abounded* toward us in wisdom. (1:8.)
8. He has *made known* to us the *mystery* of His will. (1:9.)
9. He has *sealed* us. (1:13.)

10. He has *enlightened* our understanding. (1:18.)

11. He has *raised* us to sit in heavenly places. (2:6.)

Moses was a winner, and he left us two fascinating verses in Deuteronomy 32:13,14 as he described God's dealing with His people in bringing them into greatness:

"He made him ride on the high places of the earth, that he might eat the increase of the fields; and he made him to suck honey out of the rock, and oil out of the flinty rock;"

". . . and thou didst drink the pure blood of the grape."

Picture this in your mind: ". . . *drink the pure blood of the grape.*"

You and I were born to taste the *grapes of blessing*. While some spend their lifetime discussing the size of their giants and problems, other winners dare to reach up for the grapes God promised.

There are two important principles in tasting the grapes of God:

1. THE GRAPES ARE NOT FOR THE HOLY, THEY ARE FOR THE HUNGRY.

Many people feel like they are not good enough to receive the benefits of God. But remember, ". . . *They that be whole need not a physician*" (Matt. 9:12). The Pharisees never experienced the power and the glory of the Jesus relationship. It was the Samaritan woman at the well and Zacchaeus in the tree who were hungry for His touch, His blessing, and His presence.

Maybe you have made a lot of mistakes in your life. Who hasn't? Some are perhaps more obvious! God knows your heart. He knows how desperately you want to start winning in your life. And He wants you to taste the grapes of *favor*, the grapes of *prosperity*, the grapes of *health* even more than you could ever want them!

Stop looking at your weaknesses. Start concentrating on the *strengths* He has given you. Stop looking backward. (You can't go fast looking through the rear-view mirror!)

"Oh, but Mike, you just don't know the mess I am in!" one lady cried.

"You don't drown by *falling* in the water, you drown by *staying* there," I replied.

Get up from your situation. Start setting your success in motion.

```
┌──── WISDOM PRINCIPLE ────┐
     A True Winner Will Never
            Magnify His
         Personal Weaknesses.
└──────────────────────────┘
```

2. THE GRAPES ARE NOT PLACED WITHIN YOUR MOUTH, THEY ARE PLACED WITHIN YOUR REACH.

Nobody wakes up successful and happy. Many people think, "Well, if God wanted me healthy, I'd be healthy. If God wanted me financially prosperous, I'd be that way. God is in control."

What is God in control of? He controls the *laws* of this universe. He does *not* control our *decisions!* And our decisions create and control the majority of our circumstances!

Stop assigning to the sovereignty of God the responsibility for all of your situations. Use the mind and abilities He has given you to create *new* and *better* circumstances. Go after the job He created you for. Take care of the body He has given to you. The grapes exist: but you must *reach* for them.

SEVEN GATES TO THE GRAPES

We are born to taste the grapes, born to enjoy royalty and the blessings and benefits of God. We have the *instinct for improvement*. We have a motivation for increase. *Something inside us gravitates toward growth.* We were created for *expansion*. God created us that way, and we will never be happy any other way.

I could speak forever about grapes and how beautiful they are. About the blessings of God — grapes of *wealth, health, peace, power, success* — but unless you know how to get the grapes, it will not do you any good.

1. Gate of Obedience

Deuteronomy 28:1 says, ''If thou shalt hearken diligently unto the voice of the Lord thy God . . .'' which simply means *doing what He has told you to do.* It means living up to knowledge you have received. If you are a *gallon*, live up to gallon knowledge. If you are a *pint*, live up to pint knowledge. You can move into stages of perfection and maturity as God reveals Himself to you. Abraham is called a *friend* of God *because he obeyed God.*

God said, ''Abraham, I want you to move from your comfortable situation and go to a new country,'' and Abraham *obeyed* God. If God has been talking to you about something, *do it.* Don't negotiate.

That raises a question: How can we know the voice of God? It is impossible to describe the voice of God. Oh, I could give you some guidelines, but when it comes to *knowing* when God is speaking, you have to get attached to Him. I don't have to ask, "I wonder if this lady is my mother." I know her voice. If you have spent time in the presence of God, you will know His voice.

If God is drawing you, speaking to you and dealing with you, *obey Him*. It may even appear to be a step backward. It may be something you do not want to do. But if you will say, "Father, I will do what You ask me"; if you will step through the gate of obedience, all of Heaven will open for you. God is standing by the windows of Heaven ready to pull them open and unload an avalanche of blessings if we will but obey Him. (Mal. 3:10.) He said, "If ye abide in me, and my words abide in you, ye shall ask what ye will, and it shall be done unto you" (John 15:7). Know the *power* of obedience.

2. Gate of Knowledge

God says, "My people are destroyed for lack of knowledge . . . ." (Hos. 4:6). What we do not know can destroy us. God wants us to know: *information is God's business.* All of heaven is involved in distributing information. Angels bring information. The Bible is an information manual. It is literally the *"Winner's Digest,"* informing us about God — His power, nature and thoughts about us — and about Satan, angels and demon spirits.

You have a right to the blessings of God. You are a child of the Most High God, an heir of God, a joint-heir with Jesus; He is your *elder brother.* You do have a right to enter into the Holy of Holies. You do have a *high priest*, an *intercessor* Who stands beside the right hand of the throne of God on your behalf. But you cannot take hold of the grace and blessings of God unless you have *knowledge* of what He has provided for you. I'm saying that *you have to know what belongs to you;* you must open and walk through the *gate of knowledge.*

"But without faith it is impossible to please him: for he that cometh to God must believe that he is, and that he is a rewarder of them that diligently seek him."

Hebrews 11:6

A woman came forward for prayer one night, and I asked her, "Do you want God to heal you?"

"Well," she responded, "I think He is trying to show me something."

Have you ever heard of *"Disease University?"* Many people have accepted disease and sickness as teachers. The Bible says that the *Holy Spirit will lead you into all truth.* Not, "Yea, I will send disease and it will teach you and lead you into all truth." *Know what the Word of God says, and believe it.* Pray, "God, Your Word says that You were wounded for my transgressions, bruised for my iniquities and by Your stripes I am healed." (Is. 53:5.) Claim the Word and stand upon it. You can spend your energy *explaining your sickness,* or you can spend your energy *reaching for a miracle.*

Do you have a knowledge of the grapes God has provided? Find out what the Scriptures teach; know about the grapes you are reaching for. You were born to taste the grapes, and you need to have the knowledge that God did make them available and accessible to you. A lot of people have not because they do not even know the grapes exist.

3. Gate of Visualization

Visualize the grapes. If you can not see the grapes in your mind, you will not see them in time. Your mind is a force that affects everything else in your life. *The renewing of your mind is the secret of transformation.* (Rom. 12:1,2.) Your mind is a powerful force.

The woman with the issue of blood said to herself, "If I can touch but the hem of His garment, I know I will be healed." (Mark 5:28.) She visualized. *It happened in her mind before it happened in her body.* Visualize the grapes; see yourself tasting the grapes. See yourself with victory. Some of us have never seen ourselves victorious like God means for us to see ourselves. *Visualize where God wants you to be, and then act as if you are already there.*

Jesus visualized Himself in victory: ". . . for the joy that was set before him (He) endured the cross" (Heb. 12:2). He endured the present suffering for the joy that was set before Him; His mind was picturing victory. When Jesus walked to Calvary, He was not looking at the cross; He was looking at the *resurrection.*

If you have always longed to be victorious in an area, *get your mind on the grapes* until you can visualize them and see them in your grasp. Is there a habit in your life you want to conquer? *Don't* concentrate on the habit; CONCENTRATE ON VICTORY. This is called the *law of displacement.* It means you *displace* evil by the *entrance* of good. We don't go into a building and suggest to darkness, "Would you mind leaving, because if you leave we can have light?" We bring in light, and the *entrance of light forces the exit of darkness.*

Some people spend their lives saying, "Oh, I wish I could quit thinking bad thoughts." You'll never stop thinking bad thoughts, you'll never stop thinking doubt, until you start thinking faith and you start seeing yourself victorious. That picture drives out evil. Visualize it right now. Whatever it is, see yourself with it.

4. Gate of Forgiveness

The fourth gate to the grapes is forgiveness, which simply means *the transferal of the right to judge and penalize*. It means that you give up your position on God's vengeance team. *Forgiveness does not flow to you until it can flow through you.* You can ask for forgiveness, beg God for forgiveness, offer Him "double tithe," but nothing will happen inside you until you permit God alone to penalize somebody for doing you wrong.

"Well, Mike, I want to teach him a lesson."

That's understandable, but it is wrong. God is the One in charge of payment; He is the Judge. Exercise the ability to *withhold* judgment and let God perform His program of restoration and forgiveness.

Forgiveness is the removal of information and the pain of it. There is no entry into Heaven until we walk through the gate of forgiveness. There are no grapes of blessing, no grapes of reward, until we *"remember . . . not the former things"* (Is. 43:18).

Forgive not only other people, but *forgive yourself*. That is just as important. There are people who have never forgiven themselves. *Don't advertise your mistakes.* Lay the memory of them at the cross and *leave it there.* Jesus is your sacrifice!

5. Gate of Persistence

Gate five is the gate of *persistence*. What is the gate of persistence? Simply make up your mind, regardless of how far away the grapes appear, to push on for the blessing. Sometimes it will seem like they are a thousand miles away. Friends may try to discourage and disillusion you. They may not understand your dream, your goal. It will not fall into your lap. It will not be easy. But every man or woman who has ever achieved anything had to *persist*. They made up their mind to go after what they believed in.

I met a young man the other day — sharp, nice, could be a great preacher. Will he ever be? I doubt it. Why? No persistence: "Well, I tried and it didn't work. I think I will quit. I don't know if I am called."

The power belongs to the persistent. For ten days the disciples waited in the upper room. Can you imagine the first day? Someone says, "Well, He said for us to just wait; here we are." Second day, third, fourth, fifth, sixth. Another says, "You know, if God *really* wanted us to have power, He wouldn't make us just sit here and wait for it." Seventh day. Eighth. Ninth. Tenth — suddenly, a sound from heaven as a rushing mighty wind fills the room. (Acts 2:2). Cloven tongues of fire sit upon their heads, and they began to speak in tongues as the Spirit of God gave them utterance. Why? *Persistence.*

Say it: *"Persistence."* Say it until your whole body feels it. There will be times you will not feel like you can make it. At times you will feel like asking, "Why am I doing this anyway?" Or you will feel like it's no use, nothing is going to work out. Stay there! The diseased woman didn't feel like pushing her way through the crowd, *but she had a goal.* I am certain Peter did not always feel like a big overcomer, but God gave him such a victory that when he, the man who had denied the Lord, began to preach he said, "You folk need to repent; you denied the Holy One of Israel." (Acts 2:23.) *He persisted until the power of God came into his life,* and he walked in that power.

WISDOM PRINCIPLE

Champions Simply Make
an Extra Attempt.

---

6. Gate of Sowing

You can not have grapes until you *sow* grapes. The blessing *follows* the Blesser. *Whatever good thing I do for another, God is going to do for me.* (Eph. 6:8.) If I want to taste grapes, I have to distribute grapes. I have to bless *other* people if I want God to bless *me.*

If I want something good to happen in my life, I must make something good happen for my sister or brother. I must first perform for *others* what God wants to perform for me.

Jesus did not say that if you treat your brother or sister right he or she will love you. He said that if you do right to others, *God* will do right by you. Everything reproduces after its own kind. If you want healing, start praying for *others* to experience healing. If you want blessing, start concentrating on *others' receiving* blessing. Jesus concentrated on *other* people's needs. He went around doing good, healing all that were sick and oppressed of the devil. (Acts 10:38.)

What you make happen for others, God will make happen for you.

7. Gate of Praise

The seventh gate is the gate of praise. Judah, which means *praise,* was the first tribe into battle. Praise is the sound that makes hell sick; it unnerves demons. Satan used to be the song leader in Heaven, but God kicked him out. Anytime you start praising God, all of Heaven notices it. Let the redeemed of the Lord say so; make a joyful noise; clap your hands.

Praise is an *act of the will*. It is *not* something you have to *feel* in order for it to be real. It is *not* meditation; it is something that is *heard*. Praise is articulated sound and opinion. It is your *recognition* of Jesus as Lord of everything, that Jehovah is still on the throne.

When we begin to praise God, something happens. I don't care how you feel; if you start saying, "God, I love you," something *loosens*. Talk about smashing the locks of your prison; *praise* does that! Now, praise has nothing to do with feelings. You don't have to say, "God, I feel great," or, "I feel lousy." Praise has to do with *Him* and *it takes your mind off yourself*. PRAISE LIFTS YOU TO WHERE GOD IS.

God is very comfortable with praise. In fact, that is where He chooses to *dwell*. (Ps. 22:3.) God likes praise, and He *responds* to it. Not only does God respond to praise, demons react to it.

Praise is something you deliberately *choose to do*, to acknowledge the power of God. Say, "I love You, Jesus. You're wonderful, Jesus." The purpose of praise is not just to make us feel good, but it is also so other people will hear. God enjoys advertisement! He does things in a big way. You never see God "sneaking" around saying, "You be quiet now and have a good time." He is a *celebration* God, an *expressive* God.

You were born to taste the grapes of God's blessing. The silver and gold are His. He gives us the power to get wealth. Everything that God has, everything that He is, He is willing to pour *into* us and *through* us. The grapes are not for the holy, they are for the *hungry*. They are not placed within your mouth; they are placed within your *reach*. Enter the gates and reach for the grapes. They are ACCESSIBLE.

Prayer

Lord, I thank You that You have created man to dominate and not be dominated. You have given me the opportunity to tap into Your promises and achieve the blessings and success that You want for me. I ask for Your wisdom and ability to achieve these goals, and the persistence to continue until I reach them. Thank You for equipping me to win. In Jesus' Name.

Ingredient #10
Cultivate A
Teachable Spirit

PART III

YOUR GOALS AND
HOW TO ACHIEVE THEM

YOUR GOALS
AND HOW TO
ACHIEVE THEM

One of the major causes of failure is the unwillingness to take the time to set your goals. It is also a very misunderstood practice. Some think that the Bible teaches against planning ahead, using Matthew 6:25 and James 4:13-15 as their basis. However, the concern Matthew dealt with was *worry*, not the setting of goals. James was referring to the setting of goals *without God's involvement.*

There are several reasons why some of us never set any goals for our lives. *One,* we have not been taught the power and joy of such an action. *Two,* we do not know how to go about it. *Three,* we are afraid of possible failure. (If we do not set a goal, there is no guilt nor negative feelings of not reaching it!) *Fourth,* some fail to set goals because previous failures intimidate them. Perhaps their goals were too unreasonable. At any rate, I want to help you understand the wonderful victories accomplished through WRITTEN GOALS.

In the Old Testament, Abraham's father, Terah, set a goal of making Canaan his residence. Abraham later accomplished this goal with Lot in Genesis 11,12. In the New Testament the Apostle Paul *planned* to "winter" with the Corinthians (1 Cor. 16:6) and to spend another winter in Nicopolis. (Titus 3:12.) In Proverbs 16:9 we are told: "We should make plans — counting on God to direct us (TLB). Proverbs 14:8 says: *"The wise man looks ahead . . ."* (TLB).

Planning cures disorder.

┌─ **WISDOM PRINCIPLE** ─┐

Any Disorder in Your
Life Can Create the
Death of Your Dream.

└─────────────────────┘

One outstanding lesson on planning ahead is given in Luke 14:28-30: "For which of you, intending to build a tower, sitteth not down first, and counteth the cost, whether he hath sufficient to finish it? Lest haply, after he hath laid the foundation, and is not able to finish it, all that behold it begin to mock him, Saying, This man began to build, and was not able to finish."

The setting up of specific goals is one good way of fulfilling the *purpose* God has for your life. For instance, you might *purpose* to be a better Christian this year. That is general. To fulfill that purpose, your daily goal would be to read a specific amount of chapters in the Bible *each day*, set up a *morning prayer time*, and so on.

Goal setting takes time, discipline, courage and patience. There are temptations along this line. Sometimes we let others dictate our personal goals instead of deciding for ourselves. Some people get comfortable in a particular job and stay with it for 20 years even though THEY MAY BE MISSING A DIVINE POSITION GOD IS WANTING TO TRANSFER THEM TO. Financial security to them is their job, not their Heavenly Father.

FIVE IMPORTANT STEPS

1. YOU MUST DECIDE FOR YOURSELF WHAT YOU REALLY WANT OUT OF LIFE. Nobody else can decide for you. If you don't care what happens to your life, no one will.

2. GET ALONE WITH GOD AND HIS WORD. This enables you to understand His plan and what He desires. This is getting "in agreement" with His will and purpose. This helps you to *avoid* setting the WRONG goals.

3. WRITE DOWN ON A SHEET OF PAPER EVERY SINGLE DREAM, GOAL AND DESIRE THAT IS PRESENTLY IMPORTANT TO YOU. Write down anything that you have ever wanted to DO, BECOME or POSSESS. It may be spiritual, physical, mental, financial or have to do with family, but it is important that you WRITE it down. (Do not leave it in the mind!) "The shortest pencil is better than a long memory," as my brother John has said. "Faintest line is better than strongest mind."

4. CHOOSE THE TOP THREE GOALS OUT OF THE LONG LIST. Now write down at least FIVE actions you can do NOW toward accomplishing that BIG priority goal. Remember, a BIG SUCCESS is simply several little successes linked together.

5. BE ALERT TO THE PEOPLE GOD WILL SEND INTO YOUR LIFE TO HELP YOU FULFILL HIS PURPOSE, AND BE RESPONSIVE TO OBEY GOD WHEN HE DIRECTS YOUR TALENTS TO HELP FULFILL THE DREAMS OF OTHERS. This simply restates my basic motto that God gave me during a five-day fast in 1977: "What you make happen for others, God will make happen for you."

WISDOM PRINCIPLE

The Proof of
Desire Is Pursuit.

PART IV

HOW TO ACHIEVE HAPPINESS ON YOUR JOB

HOW TO ACHIEVE
HAPPINESS
ON YOUR JOB

Is your present job a drudgery or delight?

Being on the proper job and in the right career is an important key for *total* happiness. Some blame families, their mate, their children for their frustrations, when truth would reveal that job unhappiness is "eating them up" inside.

Your work is supposed to be a source of joy!

"... to rejoice in his labour; this is the gift of God" (Eccl. 5:19). "... mine elect shall long enjoy the work of their hands" (Isa. 65:22). "The Lord shall command the blessing upon thee ... and in all that thou settest thine hand unto ..." (Deut. 28:8).

Why is your business important? It provides a sense of accomplishment that is essential for self-esteem. It *releases* your God-given *talents*. It *provides* for your family.

One of Satan's goals is to destroy your self-confidence and your sense of worth. A feeling of inadequacy can be the "cancer" that eats away your vitality and enthusiasm.

Are you unhappy with your job? Why? Is it conflict with another person? Is it lack of personal skills to do the job right? Are your God-given abilities being used *now*? Is it a "waiting room" for *eventual* promotion?

Two things you should consider. First, *you may be on the right job presently but en route to something more* suitable. Your present job could be a "temporary training ground." So, stay steady. Don't ruin friendships and your reputation through an outburst of anger or frustration. WAIT. Do your best "as unto the Lord."

Secondly, you may be on the WRONG job. Are you happy with what you are doing? Is God happy with your present work? Do you work as if God is your "boss"? Are you really giving your BEST? Be honest with yourself and do something about it! (I strongly suggest that you order a copy of my powerful booklet, *Four Forces That Guarantee Career Success* — $1.50 each . . . and change your life.)

Those who are faithful in the *little* things advance to greater. Ephesians 6:5 and 8 says: "Servants, be obedient to them that are your masters . . . . Knowing that whatsoever good thing any man doeth, the same shall he receive of the Lord . . . ."

THE WINNER AND HIS WORK

Work began in the Garden of Eden. Adam was to dress the garden and keep it. (Gen. 2:15.) This work was an activity blessed of the Lord to provide Adam with a sense of achievement and self-worth.

Then Adam sinned. His disobedience turned work into a curse: "In the sweat of thy face shalt thou eat bread, till thou return unto the ground; for out of it wast thou taken: for dust thou art, and unto dust shalt thou return" (Gen. 3:19).

Recognition of and obedience to the laws of God reinstate the blessings of work. Deuteronomy 28:8 states: "The Lord shall command the blessing upon thee in thy storehouses, and in all that thou settest thine hand unto . . ."

Many despise their jobs. Husbands lash out at their wives in frustration. Many wives arrive home work-weary and angered at the expectations of the family to "keep on working" after they get home.

If you are unhappy at work, it will affect your family life, even your health. Take time to plan your career and life's work. It deserves *your* attention. Do not accept a job based simply on convenient location, or financial sufficiency or even friendship.

FIND WHAT YOU ARE GOOD AT AND DO IT WITH ALL YOUR HEART

Be proud of what you are involved in. Never "put down" your occupation. See and cultivate an awareness of its important place in the lives of people. Strive to be the best you can be: "For which of you, intending to build a tower, sitteth not down first, and counteth the cost, whether he have sufficient to finish it?" (Luke 14:28).

CONQUERING CONFLICT ON THE JOB

One of the frustrations people face on their jobs is *people-conflict*. Anger, hostility and open resentment have caused some to leave their job prematurely.

God has really touched my spirit in this area. As a minister, many times I am in a "controlled" climate. Since I am with fellow Christians and many other top quality people most of the time, it is sometimes easy to forget the intense pressure many husbands and wives face on the everyday job.

Conflict with the boss may be caused by different reasons. He may be having personal problems at home, and is trying to compensate through job productivity. He may be experiencing the pressure of a power struggle from within the organization. He may be suppressing hostility stemming from an attitude he has discerned in you. *Talk travels!* Have you shown a rebellious attitude or expressed it to another?

Misunderstandings occur when the details of a job are not *clearly* defined. Take the time to grasp clearly what your boss or employees expect. Take nothing for granted. Aim for *quality* in your work production. Remember that God is your true manager: ''With good will doing service, as to the Lord, and not to men'' (Eph. 6:7).

KEYS FOR WINNING AT WORK!

Happiness depends on feeling good about yourself. It is based on your relationships and achievements. When your gifts and abilities are developed and utilized through your life's work, you grow in confidence and strength.

There are KEYS with which we can UNLOCK the treasures of accomplishment and confidence in our work.

1. Accept work as God's gift, not punishment.

''. . . to rejoice in his labour; this is the gift of God'' (Eccl. 5:19; also see Deut. 28:1-14).

2. Recognize God as your true employer.

''With good will doing service, as to the Lord, and not to men'' (Eph. 6:7).

3. Pursue work compatible with your abilities and interest.

"Neglect not the gift that is in thee . . ." (1 Tim. 4:14), Paul encouraged Timothy. (2 Tim. 4:5; also see Eph. 4:11.) Solomon also recognized skills. (2 Chron. 2:7-14.)

4. Learn everything possible about your job.

". . . give attendance to reading" (1 Tim. 4:13). "A wise man will hear, and will increase learning . . ." (Prov. 1:5).

5. Don't be a time thief.

"Redeeming the time, because the days are evil" (Eph. 5:16).

"Let him that stole steal no more: but rather let him labour, working with his hands the thing which is good, that he may have to give to him that needeth" (Eph. 4:28).

6. Keep a daily "need-to-do" list and establish deadlines.

". . . this one thing I do . . ." (Phil. 3:13).

"To every thing there is a season . . ." (Eccl. 3:1).

7. Ask for God's wisdom during decision-making.

"If any of you lack wisdom, let him ask of God, that giveth to all men liberally, and upbraideth not; and it shall be given him" (James 1:5).

8. Use criticism to your advantage.

In fact, get on the positive side of it: ASK your boss for suggestions and correction: "Poverty and shame shall be to him that refuseth instruction: but he that regardeth reproof shall be honoured" (Prov. 13:18).

9. Be honest about your mistakes.

"He that covereth his sins shall not prosper: but whoso confesseth and forsaketh them shall have mercy" (Prov. 28:13).

10. Be quick to ask for help and information when needed.

". . . a man of knowledge increaseth strength . . . in multitude of counsellors there is safety" (Prov. 24:5,6).

11. Assist others in their responsibilities when possible.

"Withhold not good from them to whom it is due, when it is in the power of thine hand to do it" (Prov. 3:27).

12. Project Jesus in genuine love and enthusiasm.

Resist the "holier-than-thou" attitude: ". . . the servant of the Lord must not strive; but be gentle unto all men, apt to teach, patient" (2 Tim. 2:24).

13. Do not spread gossip.

"Speak not evil one of another . . ." (James 4:11). "He that covereth a transgression seeketh love; but he that repeateth a matter separateth very friends" (Prov. 17:9). "The words of a talebearer are as wounds . . ." (Prov. 26:22). "Whoso keepeth his mouth and his tongue keepeth his soul from troubles" (Prov. 21:23).

14. Project an attitude of forgiveness, mercy and favor.

"But the wisdom that is from above is first pure, . . . full of mercy" (James 3:17). "Blessed are the merciful: for they shall obtain mercy" (Matt. 5:7).

15. Do more than is expected of you.

"And whosoever shall compel thee to go a mile, go with him twain" (Matt. 5:41).

16. Harness anger and control your spirit.

"He that hath no rule over his own spirit is like a city that is broken down, and without walls" (Prov. 25:28). "He that is soon angry dealeth foolishly..." (Prov. 14:17). "He that is slow to anger is better than the mighty; and he that ruleth his spirit than he that taketh a city" (Prov. 16:32).

17. Keep accurate records.

"Be thou diligent to know the state of thy flocks, and look well to thy herds" (Prov. 27:23).

18. Avoid flattery of others and do not give undeserved praise.

"As he that bindeth a stone in a sling, so is he that giveth honour to a fool" (Prov. 26:8). "... a flattering mouth worketh ruin" (Prov. 26:28).

19. Refuse the bondage of bribery and the influence of intimidation.

"A wicked man taketh a gift out of the bosom to pervert the ways of judgment" (Prov. 17:23). "Be not afraid of their faces: for I am with thee to deliver thee, saith the Lord" (Jer. 1:8).

20. Make Jesus your work partner.

Keep God-conscious throughout the day as you do your duties faithfully.

"Thou wilt keep him in perfect peace, whose mind is stayed on thee: because he trusteth in thee" (Isa. 26:3).

PART V

WELCOME TO A
WINNER'S WORLD

WELCOME TO A WINNER'S WORLD

I am so excited for you! The fact that you are holding this book in your hand shows *you are headed in the right direction* . . . with the *right goals* . . . and you are willing to maintain your motivation by *keeping informed.* Remember: *the difference between failure and success in life is information.* #1. Information you *receive,* #2. Information you *believe.*

As you begin to act upon this information, you will become more confident, creative and energized.

WELCOME . . .

I say, "Welcome!" because you have just entered into a new zone of happiness: victorious and successful living through Jesus Christ.

WINNER . . .

I say, "Winner," because you are exactly that! An overcomer. A conqueror. A victor!

WORLD . . .

I say, "World," because you are a new citizen in a *new domain* . . . the kingdom of God.

YOUR SUCCESS IN LIFE depends on making the right choices. There are many things in which you have *no* choice. For instance, you cannot choose your parents, nor the color of your eyes, not even the color of your skin! However, for the *important* things that really determine your happiness, *you have the right to choose!*

And may I congratulate you! YOU MADE THE RIGHT CHOICE. You chose the *right* way. The Way of hope. The Way of light. The Way of God. THE WAY OF THE WINNER! Jesus said, ''I am the way, the truth, and the life . . .'' (John 14:6).

You have received *Jesus* as your personal Savior.

You have received *forgiveness* of every past sin.

You have *crowned Him* King of your life.

You are A NEW CREATION.

In this simple step toward God, you have now discovered the *SECRET OF SUCCESS.* You are no longer a *slave* of sin, but a *son* of God!

Your decision to *experience* the Person of Jesus . . . and daily practice His principles in building a successful life reveals four beautiful qualities already inside you.

1. YOU HAVE A LOT OF AWARENESS. You *recognized* the *emptiness* in your life. You were not blind to your own inner *longing.* You knew where to find the *ANSWER.*

2. YOU HAVE A LOT OF HONESTY IN YOU. You were willing to *say,* ''God, I really need You.'' You refused to deceive yourself.

3. YOU ARE SHOWING A LOT OF COURAGE. You counted the *cost.* You were willing to pay the price. (See Luke 14:28.) Pride, past prejudices and inner fears did not stop you from total *surrender* to your Creator. That's *courage.*

4. YOU ARE USING A LOT OF FAITH ALREADY. Your faith pleases God: 1) You believe that He *exists.* 2) You believe that He *rewards.* ''But without faith it is impossible to please him: for he that cometh to God must believe that he is, and that he is a rewarder of them that diligently seek him'' (Heb. 11:6).

These qualities confirm that you are on the right road. *You have what it takes to win!* Regardless of failures and wrong decisions in the past, you have now headed in the RIGHT DIRECTION. You are in a winner's world!

TWELVE THINGS YOU CAN NOW EXPECT FROM GOD

1. HIS READY EAR TO LISTEN:

". . . thou wilt prepare their heart, thou wilt cause thine ear to hear." (Ps. 10:17). (Also see Ps. 94:9.)

2. HIS WATCHFUL EYE:

"Behold, the eye of the Lord is upon them that fear him, upon them that hope in his mercy" (Ps. 33:18). (Also see Ps. 94:9.)

3. HIS FORGIVENESS:

"If we confess our sins, he is faithful and just to forgive us our sins, and to cleanse us from all unrighteousness" (1 John 1:9). (Also see Ps. 86:5.)

4. HIS GUIDANCE:

"And the Lord shall guide thee continually, and satisfy thy soul in drought . . ." (Isa. 58:11).

5. INNER PEACE IN YOUR HEART:

"Peace I leave with you, my peace I give unto you . . ." (John 14:27.) (Also see Phil. 4:7.)

6. INNER JOY IN YOUR SPIRIT:

"Therefore with joy shall ye draw water out of the wells of salvation" (Isa. 12:3). (Also see John 15:11.)

7. HIS PROTECTION:

"There shall no evil befall thee, neither shall any plague come nigh thy dwelling" (Ps. 91:10). (Also see Ps. 32:7.)

8. NEW POWER TO OVERCOME SIN:

"Ye are of God, little children, and have overcome them: because greater is he that is in you, than he that is in the world" (1 John 4:4).(Also see Eph. 3:20.)

9. PHYSICAL HEALING IN YOU BODY:

". . . I am the Lord that healeth thee" (Ex. 15:26). (Also see Ps. 103:3 and Matt. 8:16.)

10. INNER HEALING IN YOUR BROKEN HEART:

"He healeth the broken in heart, and bindeth up their wounds" (Ps. 147:3).

"The Lord is nigh unto them that are of a broken heart; and saveth such as be of a contrite spirit" (Ps. 34:18).

11. HIS CONSISTENCY AND FAITHFULNESS:

"But the Lord is faithful, who shall establish you, and keep you from evil" (2 Thess. 3:3).

". . . lo, I am with you alway, even unto the end of the world" (Matt. 28:20).

12. HIS WISDOM FOR LIVING:

"But of him are ye in Christ Jesus, who of God is made unto us wisdom, and righteousness, and sanctification, and redemption" (1 Cor. 1:30).

POWER-KEYS YOU CAN USE

"Let us hear the conclusion of the whole matter: Fear God, and keep his commandments: for this is the whole duty of man" (Eccl. 12:13).

"He hath shewed thee, O man, what is good; and what doth the Lord require of thee, but to do justly, and to love mercy, and to walk humbly with thy God?" (Mic. 6:8).

Accepting Christ is instantaneous. However, it takes *time and discipline on your part* to become a mature and powerful believer. Here are some power keys you must remember.

SIX THINGS YOU MUST CULTIVATE

1. *God-consciousness.* Continuously center your thoughts on God and scriptural truth. This will crowd out wrong thinking, empower you during temptations and develop wisdom for important decisions.

2. *Your personal prayer life.* Set up a *place* and a daily *time* for visiting with your heavenly Father. Keep a list of names of those you pray for. Don't stay in an "asking posture" — learn to *praise* and *thank* Him for past answers!

3. *Your daily Bible reading habit.* Establish a *place*, *time* and *system*. Early morning is usually the best time because you have placed *mind-pictures* of truth into your spirit for the rest of the day. *Mark* your Bible. Take notes. Don't miss a single day.

4. *Godly friendships.* "He that walketh with wise men shall be wise: but a companion of fools shall be destroyed" (Prov. 13:20). Be *selective.* Friends will *add* *to* or *take away from* your life.

5. *A teachable spirit.* Several years ago a young lady approached me about a questionable activity in her life. She accepted my counsel. Today, she is a victorious

and successful Christian: "A wise man will hear . . ." (Prov. 1:5). Through instruction and even criticism, we grow in grace and humility.

6. *A winner's mentality.* Stop thinking about obstacles and start thinking about your *opportunities.* Talk *positive* words. Think good things about yourself and others. Stop complaining! Project enthusiasm! Avoid negative and depressing conversations. DOMINATE YOUR TURF! Be aggressively happy!

Recently, I was in a garden of beautiful flowers. While admiring their beauty, I noticed the gardener pulling up weeds that had grown up around them. As weeds choke out the life of a beautiful flower, there are things that we must remove in order to grow. To guarantee maturity and a winning life, you must eliminate the weeds.

SIX THINGS YOU MUST
ELIMINATE FROM YOUR LIFE

1. *Wrong relationships.* Ask yourself: "Will this friendship bring me *closer* to Jesus? Or will it *soil* the beauty of what God has begun?" Get rid of anything that clouds your mind or spirit.

2. *Moral impurity.* Nothing can destroy your testimony and inner joy faster than immorality. When Satan plants the "seed" of a bad thought in your mind, immediately *resist* it. Exercise your authority! Say: "Satan, I bind you and resist your ungodly suggestions. I'm a child of God walking in the power of the Holy Spirit. I cast your thought back to you. I am a new creation in Jesus!" Immediately, thank God *aloud* for good, wholesome thoughts.

3. *Ungodly mind-manipulators.* We are influenced greatly by what we *see and hear:* "Mine eye affecteth

mine heart . . ." (Lam. 3:51). Depressing television shows, sensual music and suggestive books guarantee spiritual suicide. Replace these by saturating your life and home with wholesome books, tapes and Christian materials.

4. *Negative conversation.* According to Proverbs 18:21, words minister life or death. Ephesians 4:22 says we are to *put off* the former conversation. Verse 29 instructs: "Let no corrupt communication proceed out of your mouth, but that which is good to the use of edifying, that it may minister grace unto the hearers." Psalms 50:23 says: ". . . to him that ordereth his conversation aright will I shew the salvation of God." *Insist* on positive and uplifting conversation.

5. *Bitterness and all other sin.* In Ephesians 4:31 Paul tells us: "Let all bitterness, and wrath, and anger, and clamour, and evil speaking, be put away from you . . ." Bitterness is like a cancerous sore that deteriorates the inward soul of man. Sin is the deceptive snare that poisons the possibilities of a would-be winner. It promises *roses*, but delivers *thorns.* Repent and ask God to pour out His love through you to others.

6. *Time wasters.* God is a planner. From the creation of a world in seven days, including a rest zone, to a scheduled rapture, even a marriage supper of the Lamb projected thousands of years in advance, it is easy to conclude that our Father is a Master in details, goal-setting, priorities, and order. Learn to avoid non-essentials, and energy wasters. *Make your time count:* "See then that ye walk circumspectly, not as fools, but as wise, redeeming the time, because the days are evil" (Eph. 5:15,16). Chart your course hourly. Daily. Monthly. Stay on target. Schedule every small success — literally. Time spent with *God*, time spent with *others*, and time for *yourself.*

THREE THINGS YOU MUST
CONSECRATE TO GOD

1. *Your talents and abilities.* Every human is born with God-given gifts. It is up to you to *discover* and *develop* what God gave to you. (Read Matthew 25:14-29.) *You* are responsible for *you.* Whether you possess genius in music, speaking, mechanics, sports, management, or volunteer work in a ministry . . . *you are here on purpose.* Be the *best* at what you do. Don't just put God in first place, put Him *every* place ". . . whatsoever ye do, do all to the glory of God" (1 Cor. 10:31).

2. *Job and career:* ". . . ye shall rejoice in all that ye put your hand unto . . ." (Deut. 12:7). God wants you happy with your job! If you are not excited about going to work each day, something is wrong. Does *a lack of knowledge* intimidate you? *Consult your boss* for greater understanding. *Invest time* in learning more about your field. We were made to *reach.* Like a dear friend of mine, Dr. Louis Caldwell says, "Like rubber bands, we are at our best when we are *stretched* to some degree." *Information* breeds *motivation.* On the other hand, thousands are trapped in undesirable careers through *fear.* Fear of failure, fear of the unknown. Dare to step *up and out* into new opportunities! Dare to try! *The dreamer, the achiever, the adventurer is destined for supernatural success.*

3. *Your money.* Money talks. It reveals your true values. Jesus talked about it. The Apostle Paul talked about it. Money is *important.* It is your time, your toil, your sweat, your energy . . . it is *you.* It is the *power part* of you. With it you bargain and exchange your way through life. It is *your food.* Your *shelter.* Your *clothing.* *What you do with it makes all the difference in the world*

to God. Abraham gave 10% to God in thanksgiving for His blessing. In Matthew 23:23 Jesus commended the Pharisees for doing the same. Tithing is *not* the payment of a debt to God. All of it belongs to Him. Tithing is the *acknowledgement* of the debt. Offerings to God are seeds planted in holy soil; and He personally guarantees a bountiful return. (Read Deut. 8:18; Deut. 28:1-14; Luke 6:38, 2 Cor. 9:6; Mal. 3:10,11.)

TWO SUCCESS-FORCES YOU MUST ACTIVATE

1. *Your words:* "The mouth of the just bringeth forth wisdom . . ." (Prov. 10:31). ". . . he that winneth souls is wise" (Prov. 11:30). Proverbs 10:20 says: "The tongue of the just is as choice silver . . ."

WORDS HAVE POWER. Men talk about the things they *love* whether it be football, children or pizza! True born-again believers thrive on God-talk! You should want to talk about the promises and power of God to Christians and non-Christians alike.

The secrets of man will surface through the mouth. Matthew 12:34 says: ". . . out of the abundance of the heart the mouth speaketh." Dare to speak out to others about what God has done in your life: "Let the redeemed of the Lord SAY so . . ." (Ps. 107:2). Tell your family. Your friends. Your fellow workers. With gentle, loving and kind words, portray with authority the life of Jesus within you.

2. *Your relationship:* "He that walketh with wise men shall be wise . . ." (Prov. 13:20).

Identify and associate with quality people. This is one of the great secrets of success. Surround yourself with a "Success-Climate" of Jesus-lovers. You need to have a church "home." For growth, stability and ministry

God established the local church and pastor for your own spiritual success. Do not select a church based only upon friendships, convenience or traditions. *Seek God.* Listen to the Holy Spirit. *He knows where He can use you best.* Be loyal and committed to that congregation. In attendance, involvement and financial support, *stand behind that pastor* with your faithfulness.

WISDOM PRINCIPLE

Tomorrow Contains More
Joy Than Any Yesterday
You Can Recall.

A FINAL WORD

Read this book at least once a week for the next few months. As it gets into your mind and spirit, your spiritual growth will amaze you! A dynamic vitality will develop that will astound even your friends. YOU TRULY WILL BE A WINNER.

My own goal in life as a minister of the gospel of Jesus Christ is to make others successful. Please feel free to write me and share your prayer needs. I believe and practice the power of daily prayer. I will pray for you, I will write you back and tell you what I feel God wants you to know.

PART VI

READING THE BIBLE
IN ONE YEAR:
A COMPLETE PROGRAM

January

1 Gen. 1-2; Ps. 1; Matt. 1-2
2 Gen. 3-4; Ps. 2; Matt. 3-4
3 Gen. 5-7; Ps. 3; Matt. 5
4 Gen. 8-9; Ps. 4; Matt. 6-7
5 Gen. 10-11; Ps. 5; Matt. 8-9
6 Gen. 12-13; Ps. 6; Matt. 10-11
7 Gen. 14-15; Ps. 7; Matt. 12
8 Gen. 16-17; Ps. 8; Matt. 13
9 Gen. 18-19; Ps. 9; Matt. 14-15
10 Gen. 20-21; Ps. 10; Matt. 16 17
11 Gen. 22-23; Ps. 11; Matt. 18
12 Gen. 24; Ps. 12; Matt. 19-20
13 Gen. 25-26; Ps. 13; Matt. 21
14 Gen. 27-28; Ps. 14; Matt. 22
15 Gen. 29-30; Ps. 15; Matt. 23
16 Gen. 31-32; Ps. 16; Matt. 24
17 Gen. 33-34; Ps. 17; Matt. 25
18 Gen. 35-36; Ps. 18; Matt. 26
19 Gen. 37-38; Ps. 19; Matt. 27
20 Gen. 39-40; Ps. 20; Matt. 28
21 Gen. 41-42; Ps. 21; Mark 1
22 Gen. 43-44; Ps. 22; Mark 2
23 Gen. 45-46; Ps. 23; Mark 3
24 Gen. 47-48; Ps. 24; Mark 4
25 Gen. 49-50; Ps. 25; Mark 5
26 Ex. 1-2; Ps. 26; Mark 6
27 Ex. 3-4; Ps. 27; Mark 7
28 Ex. 5-6; Ps. 28; Mark 8
29 Ex. 7-8; Ps. 29; Mark 9
30 Ex. 9-10; Ps. 30; Mark 10
31 Ex. 11-12; Ps. 31; Mark 11

February

1   Ex. 13-14; Ps. 32; Mark 12
2   Ex. 15-16; Ps. 33; Mark 13
3   Ex. 17-18; Ps. 34; Mark 14
4   Ex. 19-20; Ps. 35; Mark 15
5   Ex. 21-22; Ps. 36; Mark 16
6   Ex. 23-24; Ps. 37; Luke 1
7   Ex. 25-26; Ps. 38; Luke 2
8   Ex. 27-28; Ps. 39; Luke 3
9   Ex. 29-30; Ps. 40; Luke 4
10   Ex. 31-32; Ps. 41; Luke 5
11   Ex. 33-34; Ps. 42; Luke 6
12   Ex. 35-36; Ps. 43; Luke 7
13   Ex. 37-38; Ps. 44; Luke 8
14   Ex. 39-40; Ps. 45; Luke 9
15   Lev. 1-2; Ps. 46; Luke 10
16   Lev. 3-4; Ps. 47; Luke 11
17   Lev. 5-6; Ps. 48; Luke 12
18   Lev. 7-8; Ps. 49; Luke 13
19   Lev. 9-10; Ps. 50; Luke 14
20   Lev. 11-12; Ps. 51; Luke 15
21   Lev. 13; Ps. 52; Luke 16
22   Lev. 14; Ps. 53; Luke 17
23   Lev. 15-16; Ps. 54; Luke 18
24   Lev. 17-18; Ps. 55; Luke 19
25   Lev. 19-20; Ps. 56; Luke 20
26   Lev. 21-22; Ps. 57; Luke 21
27   Lev. 23-24; Ps. 58; Luke 22
28   Lev. 25
29   Ps. 59; Luke 23

March

1 Lev. 26-27; Ps. 60; Luke 24
2 Num. 1-2; Ps. 61; John 1
3 Num. 3-4; Ps. 62; John 2-3
4 Num. 5-6; Ps. 63; John 4
5 Num. 7; Ps. 64; John 5
6 Num. 8-9; Ps. 65; John 6
7 Num. 10-11; Ps. 66; John 7
8 Num. 12-13; Ps. 67; John 8
9 Num. 14-15; Ps. 68; John 9
10 Num. 16; Ps. 69; John 10
11 Num. 17-18; Ps. 70; John 11
12 Num. 19-20; Ps. 71; John 12
13 Num. 21-22; Ps. 72; John 13
14 Num. 23-24; Ps. 73; John 14-15
15 Num. 25-26; Ps. 74; John 16
16 Num. 27-28; Ps. 75; John 17
17 Num. 29-30; Ps. 76; John 18
18 Num. 31-32; Ps. 77; John 19
19 Num. 33-34; Ps. 78; John 20
20 Num. 35-36; Ps. 79; John 21
21 Deut. 1-2; Ps. 80; Acts 1
22 Deut. 3-4; Ps. 81; Acts 2
23 Deut. 5-6; Ps. 82; Acts 3-4
24 Deut. 7-8; Ps. 83; Acts 5-6
25 Deut. 9-10; Ps. 84; Acts 7
26 Deut. 11-12; Ps. 85; Acts 8
27 Deut. 13-14; Ps. 86; Acts 9
28 Deut. 15-16; Ps. 87; Acts 10
29 Deut. 17-18; Ps. 88; Acts 11-12
30 Deut. 19-20; Ps. 89; Acts 13
31 Deut. 21-22; Ps. 90; Acts 14

April

1   Deut. 23-24; Ps. 91; Acts 15
2   Deut. 25-27; Ps. 92; Acts 16
3   Deut. 28-29; Ps. 93; Acts 17
4   Deut. 30-31; Ps. 94; Acts 18
5   Deut. 32; Ps. 95; Acts 19
6   Deut. 33-34; Ps. 96; Acts 20
7   Josh. 1-2; Ps. 97; Acts 21
8   Josh. 3-4; Ps. 98; Acts 22
9   Josh. 5-6; Ps. 99; Acts 23
10 Josh. 7-8; Ps. 100; Acts 24-25
11 Josh. 9-10; Ps. 101; Acts 26
12 Josh. 11-12; Ps. 102; Acts 27
13 Josh. 13-14; Ps. 103; Acts 28
14 Josh. 15-16; Ps. 104; Rom. 1-2
15 Josh. 17-18; Ps. 105; Rom. 3-4
16 Josh. 19-20; Ps. 106; Rom. 5-6
17 Josh. 21-22; Ps. 107; Rom. 7-8
18 Josh. 23-24; Ps. 108; Rom. 9-10
19 Judg. 1-2; Ps. 109; Rom. 11-12
20 Judg. 3-4; Ps. 110; Rom. 13-14
21 Judg. 5-6; Ps. 111; Rom. 15-16
22 Judg. 7-8; Ps. 112; 1 Cor. 1-2
23 Judg. 9; Ps. 113; 1 Cor. 3-4
24 Judg. 10-11; Ps. 114; 1 Cor. 5-6
25 Judg. 12-13; Ps. 115; 1 Cor. 7
26 Judg. 14-15; Ps. 116; 1 Cor. 8-9
27 Judg. 16-17; Ps. 117; 1 Cor. 10
28 Judg. 18-19; Ps. 118; 1 Cor. 11
29 Judg. 20-21; Ps. 119:1-88; 1 Cor. 12
30 Ruth 1-4; Ps. 119:89-176; 1 Cor. 13

May

1   1 Sam. 1-2; Ps. 120; 1 Cor. 14
2   1 Sam. 3-4; Ps. 121; 1 Cor. 15
3   1 Sam. 5-6; Ps. 122; 1 Cor. 16
4   1 Sam. 7-8; Ps. 123; 2 Cor. 1
5   1 Sam. 9-10; Ps. 124; 2 Cor. 2-3
6   1 Sam. 11-12; Ps. 125; 2 Cor. 4-5
7   1 Sam. 13-14; Ps. 126; 2 Cor. 6-7
8   1 Sam. 15-16; Ps. 127; 2 Cor. 8
9   1 Sam. 17; Ps. 128; 2 Cor. 9-10
10   1 Sam. 18-19; Ps. 129; 2 Cor. 11
11   1 Sam. 20-21; Ps. 130; 2 Cor. 12
12   1 Sam. 22-23; Ps. 131; 2 Cor. 13
13   1 Sam. 24-25; Ps. 132; Gal. 1-2
14   1 Sam. 26-27; Ps. 133; Gal. 3-4
15   1 Sam. 28-29; Ps. 134; Gal. 5-6
16   1 Sam. 30-31; Ps. 135; Eph. 1-2
17   2 Sam. 1-2; Ps. 136; Eph. 3-4
18   2 Sam. 3-4; Ps. 137; Eph. 5-6
19   2 Sam. 5-6; Ps. 138; Phil. 1-2
20   2 Sam. 7-8; Ps. 139; Phil. 3-4
21   2 Sam. 9-10; Ps. 140; Col. 1-2
22   2 Sam. 11-12; Ps. 141; Col. 3-4
23   2 Sam. 13-14; Ps. 142; 1 Thess. 1-2
24   2 Sam. 15-16; Ps. 143; 1 Thess. 3-4
25   2 Sam. 17-18; Ps. 144; 1 Thess. 5
26   2 Sam. 19; Ps. 145; 2 Thess. 1-3
27   2 Sam. 20-21; Ps. 146; 1 Tim. 1-2
28   2 Sam. 22; Ps. 147; 1 Tim. 3-4
29   2 Sam. 23-24; Ps. 148; 1 Tim. 5-6
30   1 Kings 1; Ps. 149; 2 Tim. 1-2
31   1 Kings 2-3; Ps. 150; 2 Tim. 3-4

June

1   1 Kings 4-5; Prov. 1; Titus 1-3
2   1 Kings 6-7; Prov. 2; Philem.
3   1 Kings 8; Prov. 3; Heb. 1-2
4   1 Kings 9-10; Prov. 4; Heb. 3-4
5   1 Kings 11-12; Prov. 5; Heb. 5-6
6   1 Kings 13-14; Prov. 6; Heb. 7-8
7   1 Kings 15-16; Prov. 7; Heb. 9-10
8   1 Kings 17-18; Prov. 8; Heb. 11
9   1 Kings 19-20; Prov. 9; Heb. 12
10 1 Kings 21-22; Prov. 10; Heb. 13
11 2 Kings 1-2; Prov. 11; James 1
12 2 Kings 3-4; Prov. 12; James 2-3
13 2 Kings 5-6; Prov. 13; James 4-5
14 2 Kings 7-8; Prov. 14; 1 Pet. 1
15 2 Kings 9-10; Prov. 15; 1 Pet. 2-3
16 2 Kings 11-12; Prov. 16; 1 Pet. 4-5
17 2 Kings 13-14; Prov. 17; 2 Pet. 1-3
18 2 Kings 15-16; Prov. 18; 1 John 1-2
19 2 Kings 17; Prov. 19; 1 John 3-4
20 2 Kings 18-19; Prov. 20; 1 John 5
21 2 Kings 20-21; Prov. 21; 2 John
22 2 Kings 22-23; Prov. 22; 3 John
23 2 Kings 24-25; Prov. 23; Jude
24 1 Chron. 1; Prov. 24; Rev. 1-2
25 1 Chron. 2-3; Prov. 25; Rev. 3-5
26 1 Chron. 4-5; Prov. 26; Rev. 6-7
27 1 Chron. 6-7; Prov. 27; Rev. 8-10
28 1 Chron. 8-9; Prov. 28; Rev. 11-12
29 1 Chron. 10-11; Prov. 29; Rev. 13-14
30 1 Chron. 12-13; Prov. 30; Rev. 15-17

July

1 1 Chron. 14-15; Prov. 31; Rev. 18-19
2 1 Chron. 16-17; Ps. 1; Rev. 20-22
3 1 Chron. 18-19; Ps. 2; Matt. 1-2
4 1 Chron. 20-21; Ps. 3; Matt. 3-4
5 1 Chron. 22-23; Ps. 4; Matt. 5
6 1 Chron. 24-25; Ps. 5; Matt. 6-7
7 1 Chron. 26-27; Ps. 6; Matt. 8-9
8 1 Chron. 28-29; Ps. 7; Matt. 10-11
9 2 Chron. 1-2; Ps. 8; Matt. 12
10 2 Chron. 3-4; Ps. 9; Matt. 13
11 2 Chron. 5-6; Ps. 10; Matt. 14-15
12 2 Chron. 7-8; Ps. 11; Matt. 16-17
13 2 Chron. 9-10; Ps. 12; Matt. 18
14 2 Chron. 11-12; Ps. 13; Matt. 19-20
15 2 Chron. 13-14; Ps. 14; Matt. 21
16 2 Chron. 15-16; Ps. 15; Matt. 22
17 2 Chron. 17-18; Ps. 16; Matt. 23
18 2 Chron. 19-20; Ps. 17; Matt. 24
19 2 Chron. 21-22; Ps. 18; Matt. 25
20 2 Chron. 23-24; Ps. 19; Matt. 26
21 2 Chron. 25-26; Ps. 20; Matt. 27
22 2 Chron. 27-28; Ps. 21; Matt. 28
23 2 Chron. 29-30; Ps. 22; Mark 1
24 2 Chron. 31-32; Ps. 23; Mark 2
25 2 Chron. 33-34; Ps. 24; Mark 3
26 2 Chron. 35-36; Ps. 25; Mark 4
27 Ezra 1-2; Ps. 26; Mark 5
28 Ezra 3-4; Ps. 27; Mark 6
29 Ezra 5-6; Ps. 28; Mark 7
30 Ezra 7-8; Ps. 29; Mark 8
31 Ezra 9-10; Ps. 30; Mark 9

August

1 Neh. 1-2; Ps. 31; Mark 10
2 Neh. 3-4; Ps. 32; Mark 11
3 Neh. 5-6; Ps. 33; Mark 12
4 Neh. 7, Ps. 34; Mark 13
5 Neh. 8-9; Ps. 35; Mark 14
6 Neh. 10-11; Ps. 36; Mark 15
7 Neh. 12-13; Ps. 37; Mark 16
8 Esth. 1-2; Ps. 38; Luke 1
9 Esth. 3-4; Ps. 39; Luke 2
10 Esth. 5-6; Ps. 40; Luke 3
11 Esth. 7-8; Ps. 41; Luke 4
12 Esth. 9-10; Ps. 42; Luke 5
13 Job 1-2; Ps. 43; Luke 6
14 Job 3-4; Ps. 44; Luke 7
15 Job 5-6; Ps. 45; Luke 8
16 Job 7-8; Ps. 46; Luke 9
17 Job 9-10; Ps. 47; Luke 10
18 Job 11-12; Ps. 48; Luke 11
19 Job 13-14; Ps. 49; Luke 12
20 Job 15-16; Ps. 50; Luke 13
21 Job 17-18; Ps. 51; Luke 14
22 Job 19-20; Ps. 52; Luke 15
23 Job 21-22; Ps. 53; Luke 16
24 Job 23-25; Ps. 54; Luke 17
25 Job 26-28; Ps. 55; Luke 18
26 Job 29-30; Ps. 56; Luke 19
27 Job 31-32; Ps. 57; Luke 20
28 Job 33-34; Ps. 58; Luke 21
29 Job 35-36; Ps. 59; Luke 22
30 Job 37-38; Ps. 60; Luke 23
31 Job 39-40; Ps. 61; Luke 24

September

1   Job 41-42; Ps. 62; John 1
2   Eccl. 1-2; Ps. 63; John 2-3
3   Eccl. 3-4; Ps. 64; John 4
4   Eccl. 5-6; Ps. 65; John 5
5   Eccl. 7-8; Ps. 66; John 6
6   Eccl. 9-10; Ps. 67; John 7
7   Eccl. 11-12; Ps. 68; John 8
8   Song of Sol. 1-2; Ps. 69; John 9
9   Song of Sol. 3-4; Ps. 70; John 10
10 Song of Sol. 5-6; Ps. 71; John 11
11 Song of Sol. 7-8; Ps. 72; John 12
12 Isaiah 1-2; Ps. 73; John 13
13 Isaiah 3-5; Ps. 74; John 14-15
14 Isaiah 6-8; Ps. 75; John 16
15 Isaiah 9-10; Ps. 76; John 17
16 Isaiah 11-13; Ps. 77; John 18
17 Isaiah 14-15; Ps. 78; John 19
18 Isaiah 16-17; Ps. 79; John 20
19 Isaiah 18-19; Ps. 80; John 21
20 Isaiah 20-22; Ps. 81; Acts 1
21 Isaiah 23-24; Ps. 82; Acts 2
22 Isaiah 25-26; Ps. 83; Acts 3-4
23 Isaiah 27-28; Ps. 84; Acts 5-6
24 Isaiah 29-30; Ps. 85; Acts 7
25 Isaiah 31-32; Ps. 86; Acts 8
26 Isaiah 33-34; Ps. 87; Acts 9
27 Isaiah 35-36; Ps. 88; Acts 10
28 Isaiah 37-38; Ps. 89; Acts 11-12
29 Isaiah 39-40; Ps. 90; Acts 13
30 Isaiah 41-42; Ps. 91; Acts 14

October

1   Isaiah 43-44; Ps. 92; Acts 15
2   Isaiah 45-46; Ps. 93; Acts 16
3   Isaiah 47-48; Ps. 94; Acts 17
4   Isaiah 49-50; Ps. 95; Acts 18
5   Isaiah 51-52; Ps. 96; Acts 19
6   Isaiah 53-54; Ps. 97; Acts 20
7   Isaiah 55-56; Ps. 98; Acts 21
8   Isaiah 57-58; Ps. 99; Acts 22
9   Isaiah 59-60; Ps. 100; Acts 23
10   Isaiah 61-62; Ps. 101; Acts 24-25
11   Isaiah 63-64; Ps. 102; Acts 26
12   Isaiah 65-66; Ps. 103; Acts 27
13   Jer. 1-2; Ps. 104; Acts 28
14   Jer. 3-4; Ps. 105; Rom. 1-2
15   Jer. 5-6; Ps. 106; Rom. 3-4
16   Jer. 7-8; Ps. 107; Rom. 5-6
17   Jer. 9-10; Ps. 108; Rom. 7-8
18   Jer. 11-12; Ps. 109; Rom. 9-10
19   Jer. 13-14; Ps. 110; Rom. 11-12
20   Jer. 15-16; Ps. 111; Rom. 13-14
21   Jer. 17-18; Ps. 112; Rom. 15-16
22   Jer. 19-20; Ps. 113; 1 Cor. 1-2
23   Jer. 21-22; Ps. 114; 1 Cor. 3-4
24   Jer. 23-24; Ps. 115; 1 Cor. 5-6
25   Jer. 25-26; Ps. 116; 1 Cor. 7
26   Jer. 27-28; Ps. 117; 1 Cor. 8-9
27   Jer. 29-30; Ps. 118; 1 Cor. 10
28   Jer. 31-32; Ps. 119:1-64; 1 Cor. 11
29   Jer. 33-34; Ps. 119:65-120; 1 Cor. 12
30   Jer. 35-36; Ps. 119:121-176; 1 Cor. 13
31   Jer. 37-38; Ps. 120; 1 Cor. 14

November

1   Jer. 39-40; Ps. 121; 1 Cor. 15
2   Jer. 41-42; Ps. 122; 1 Cor. 16
3   Jer. 43-44; Ps. 123; 2 Cor. 1
4   Jer. 45-46; Ps. 124; 2 Cor. 2-3
5   Jer. 47-48; Ps. 125; 2 Cor. 4-5
6   Jer. 49-50; Ps. 126; 2 Cor. 6-7
7   Jer. 51-52; Ps. 127; 2 Cor. 8
8   Lam. 1-2; Ps. 128; 2 Cor. 9-10
9   Lam. 3; Ps. 129; 2 Cor. 11
10 Lam. 4-5; Ps. 130; 2 Cor. 12
11 Ezek. 1-2; Ps. 131; 2 Cor. 13
12 Ezek. 3-4; Ps. 132; Gal. 1-2
13 Ezek. 5-6; Ps. 133; Gal. 3-4
14 Ezek. 7-8; Ps. 134; Gal. 5-6
15 Ezek. 9-10; Ps. 135; Eph. 1-2
16 Ezek. 11-12; Ps. 136; Eph. 3-4
17 Ezek. 13-14; Ps. 137; Eph. 5-6
18 Ezek. 15-16; Ps. 138; Phil. 1-2
19 Ezek. 17-18; Ps. 139; Phil. 3-4
20 Ezek. 19-20; Ps. 140; Col. 1-2
21 Ezek. 21-22; Ps. 141; Col. 3-4
22 Ezek. 23-24; Ps. 142; 1 Thess. 1-2
23 Ezek. 25-26; Ps. 143; 1 Thess. 3-4
24 Ezek. 27-28; Ps. 144; 1 Thess. 5
25 Ezek. 29-30; Ps. 145; 2 Thess. 1-3
26 Ezek. 31-32; Ps. 146; 1 Tim. 1-2
27 Ezek. 33-34; Ps. 147; 1 Tim. 3-4
28 Ezek. 35-36; Ps. 148; 1 Tim. 5-6
29 Ezek. 37-38; Ps. 149; 2 Tim. 1-2
30 Ezek. 39-40; Ps. 150; 2 Tim. 3-4

December

1 Ezek. 41-42; Prov. 1; Titus 1-3
2 Ezek. 43-44; Prov. 2; Philem.
3 Ezek. 45-46; Prov. 3; Heb. 1-2
4 Ezek. 47-48; Prov. 4; Heb. 3-4
5 Dan. 1-2; Prov. 5; Heb. 5-6
6 Dan. 3-4; Prov. 6; Heb. 7-8
7 Dan. 5-6; Prov. 7; Heb. 9-10
8 Dan. 7-8; Prov. 8; Heb. 11
9 Dan. 9-10; Prov. 9; Heb. 12
10 Dan. 11-12; Prov. 10; Heb. 13
11 Hos. 1-3; Prov. 11; James 1-3
12 Hos. 4-6; Prov. 12; James 4-5
13 Hos. 7-8; Prov. 13; 1 Pet. 1
14 Hos. 9-11; Prov. 14; 1 Pet. 2-3
15 Hos. 12-14; Prov. 15; 1 Pet. 4-5
16 Joel 1-3; Prov. 16; 2 Pet. 1-3
17 Amos 1-3; Prov. 17; 1 John 1-2
18 Amos 4-6; Prov. 18; 1 John 3-4
19 Amos 7-9; Prov. 19; 1 John 5
20 Obad.; Prov. 20; 2 John
21 Jonah 1-4; Prov. 21; 3 John
22 Mic. 1-4; Prov. 22; Jude
23 Mic. 5-7; Prov. 23; Rev. 1-2
24 Nah. 1-3; Prov. 24; Rev. 3-5
25 Hab. 1-3; Prov. 25; Rev. 6-7
26 Zeph. 1-3; Prov. 26; Rev. 8-10
27 Hag. 1-2; Prov. 27; Rev. 11-12
28 Zech. 1-4; Prov. 28; Rev. 13-14
29 Zech. 5-9; Prov. 29; Rev. 15-17
30 Zech. 10-14; Prov. 30; Rev. 18-19
31 Mal. 1-4; Prov. 31; Rev. 20-22

DECISION PAGE

MAY I INVITE YOU TO MAKE JESUS CHRIST THE LORD OF YOUR LIFE?

The Bible says, "That if thou shalt confess with thy mouth the Lord Jesus, and shalt believe in thine heart that God hath raised him from the dead, thou shalt be saved. For with the heart man believeth unto righteousness; and with the mouth confession is made unto salvation" (Romans 10:9-10).

To receive Jesus Christ as Lord and Savior of your life, please pray this prayer from your heart today!

"Dear Jesus, I believe that You died for me and rose again on the third day. I confess to You that I am a sinner. I need Your love and forgiveness. Come into my life, forgive my sins, and give me eternal life. I confess You now as my Lord. Thank You for my salvation! I walk in Your peace and joy from this day forward. Amen."

Signed _____

Date _____

Return this today!

☐ Yes, Mike! I made a decision to accept Christ as my personal Savior today. Please send more information to help me with my new life in Christ.   PD01

Miss
Mrs.
Name Mr._____
                        Please Print

Address _____

City _____

State _____

Zip _____

Phone ( ) _____
                                                    DC07

Mail to:
Dr. Mike Murdock • P.O. Box 99 • Dallas, Texas 75221

Additional copies of
*The One Minute
Businessman's Devotional*
and other books
by Mike Murdock
are available from your local bookstore
or from:

P. O. Box 55388
Tulsa, OK 74155

STUDY NOTES

STUDY NOTES

STUDY NOTES

_____

_____

_____

_____

_____

_____

_____

_____

_____

_____

_____

_____

_____

_____

_____

_____

_____

_____

_____

_____

_____

_____

STUDY NOTES

STUDY NOTES

STUDY NOTES

STUDY NOTES

STUDY NOTES

STUDY NOTES

STUDY NOTES

STUDY NOTES

_____
_____
_____
_____
_____
_____
_____
_____
_____
_____
_____
_____
_____
_____
_____
_____
_____
_____
_____
_____
_____
_____
_____
_____

STUDY NOTES

STUDY NOTES

STUDY NOTES

STUDY NOTES

STUDY NOTES